The End of the Roman Empire

PROBLEMS IN EUROPEAN
CIVILIZATION SERIES

The End of the Roman Empire

Decline or Transformation?

Third Edition

Edited and with an introduction by
Donald Kagan
Yale University

D. C. HEATH AND COMPANY
Lexington, Massachusetts Toronto

Address editorial correspondence to:

D. C. Heath
125 Spring Street
Lexington, MA 02173

Acquisitions Editor: James Miller
Production Editor: Cormac Joseph Morrissey
Designer: Alwyn R. Velásquez
Production Coordinator: Charles Dutton
Photo Researcher: Martha Friedman
Text Permissions Editor: Margaret Roll

Published simultaneously in Canada.

Printed in the United States of America.

International Standard Book Number: 0-669-21520-1

Library of Congress Catalog Number: 91-70715

10 9 8 7 6 5 4 3 2 1

Contents

Chronology of Events

ca. 4 B.C.	Jesus of Nazareth born
27 B.C.–A.D. 14	Augustus
14–37	Tiberius
ca. 30	Crucifixion of Jesus
37–41	Gaius (Caligula)
41–54	Claudius
54–68	Nero
	Fire at Rome—Persecution by Nero
69	Year of the Four Emperors
ca. 70–100	Gospels written
69–79	Vespasian
79–81	Titus
81–96	Domitian
96–98	Nerva
98–117	Trajan
117–138	Hadrian
138–161	Antoninus Pius
161–180	Marcus Aurelius
180–192	Commodus
193–211	Septimius Severus
222–235	Alexander Severus
ca. 250–260	Major persecutions by Decius and Valerian

249–251	Decius
253–260	Valerian
253–268	Gallienus
268–270	Claudius II Gothicus
270–275	Aurelian
284–305	Diocletian
303	Persecution by Diocletian
306–337	Constantine
311	Gallienus issues Edict of Toleration
312	Battle of Milvian Bridge—Conversion of Constantine to Christianity
324–337	Constantine sole emperor
325	Council of Nicaea
337–361	Constantius II
361–363	Julian the Apostate
364–375	Valentinian
364–378	Valens
379–395	Theodosius
395	Christianity becomes official religion of Roman Empire

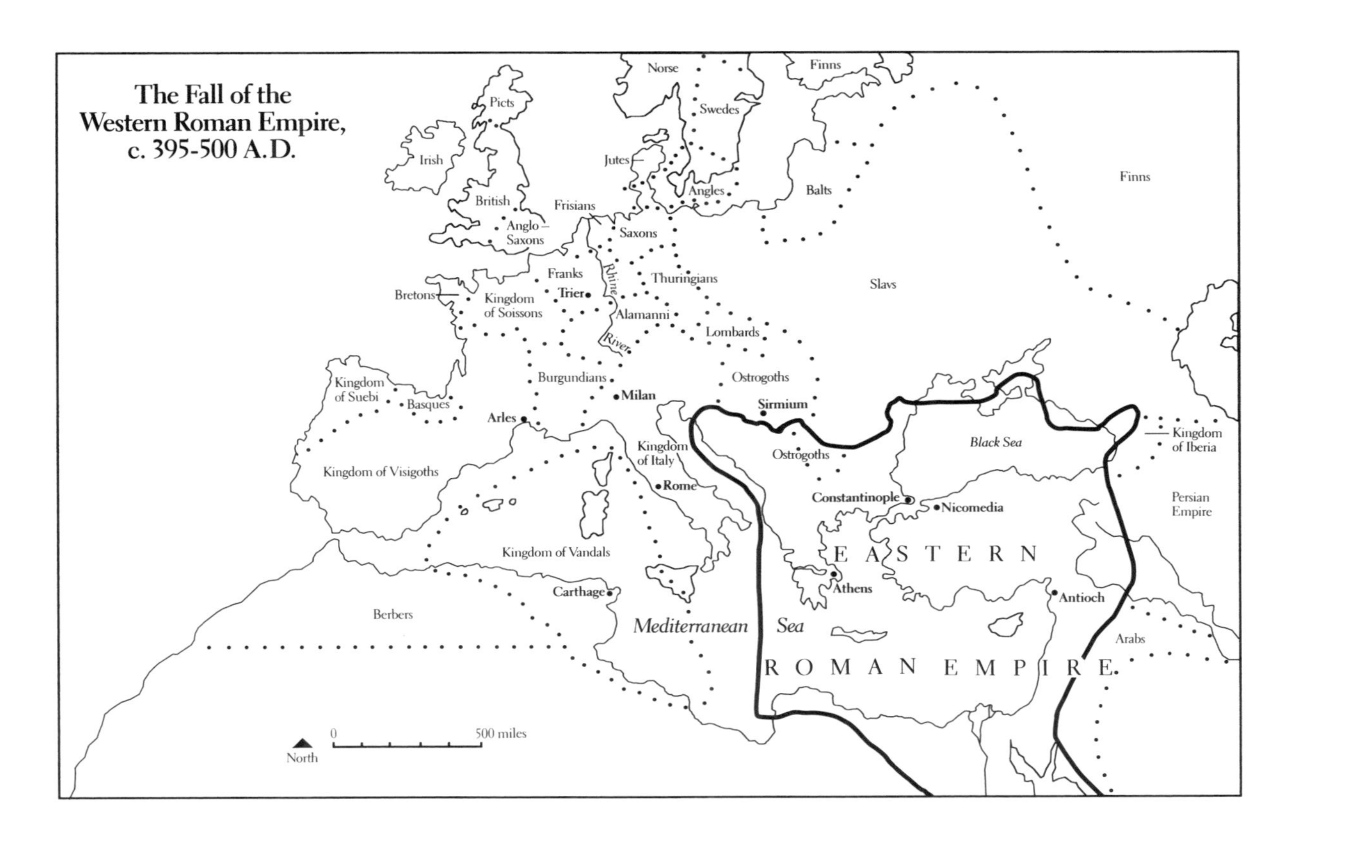
The Fall of the
Western Roman Empire,
c. 395-500 A.D.
Norse
Finns
Swedes
Picts
Irish
Jutes
Angles
Balts
Finns
British
Frisians
Anglo-Saxons
Saxons
Franks
Rhine River
Thuringians
Slavs
Bretons
Kingdom of Soissons
Trier
Alamanni
Lombards
Burgundians
Ostrogoths
Kingdom of Suebi
Basques
Milan
Sirmium
Arles
Kingdom of Italy
Black Sea
Kingdom of Iberia
Ostrogoths
Kingdom of Visigoths
Rome
Constantinople
Nicomedia
Persian Empire
Kingdom of Vandals
EASTERN
Athens
Carthage
Antioch
Berbers
Mediterranean Sea
Arabs
ROMAN EMPIRE
0
500 miles
North

Introduction

Among the historical questions that have been posed through the ages, none has attracted more attention over a longer period of time than the one that asks, Why did the Roman Empire in the West collapse? It has remained a vital question because each age has seen in the tale of Rome's fall something significant and relevant to its own situation. The theme has been especially attractive in our own time; the fate of Rome looms large in the cosmic speculation of Spengler and Toynbee and has been intensively treated from countless points of view. The first treatment of the decline of Rome as an historical problem had to wait until the Renaissance, when the Humanists became aware of their own break with the medieval period and, therefore, of the break between the Middle Ages and classical antiquity. Whether they blamed internal failures, as did Petrarch, or the barbarian attacks, as did Machiavelli, they were the first to show awareness of the problem.

The selections in Part I attempt to define the problem. Michael I. Rostovtzeff divides the concept of decline into two major divisions: (1) political, economic, and social, and (2) intellectual and spiritual. For him the Roman Empire's decline meant the barbarization of political institutions, the simplification and localization of economic functions, the decay and disappearance of urban life, and, in the intellectual and spiritual sphere, the development among the masses of a mentality "based exclusively on religion and not only indifferent but hostile to the intellectual achievements of the higher classes." F. W. Walbank helps clarify the problem by setting it in its historical perspective and by defining the field of inquiry proper to it: "When we say a society is in decay, we refer to something having gone wrong within its structure, or in the relationship between the various groups which compose it." A. H. M. Jones sees the problem in more simple, material terms and calls attention to the survival of the eastern half of the empire a millennium after the collapse in the West.

Part II offers a selection of some of the explanations given for Rome's decay and collapse. A glance at them reveals the great variety of ways of seeing the problem and the forbidding difficulties standing in the way of consensus. To begin with, the usual categories of explanation — political, economic, social, or moral — prove none too helpful, for all played some role, and rare is the explanation that fixes on one to the total exclusion of the others. The Rostovtzeff thesis, for example, uses all these categories to make its point of the barbarization of Rome by the absorption of the educated classes by the masses.

It may, therefore, be more useful to classify the solutions differently. Let students of Rome's decline imagine themselves as medical examiners who have been confronted with a corpse. It is their duty to establish first the time of death and then the cause. It soon becomes apparent that the various historical practitioners who have examined the Roman remains have achieved remarkably little agreement on either question. The general view has been that Rome reached its peak in the second century of the Christian era under its Antonine monarchs; it grew ill during the upheavals of the third century, suffered hardening of the arteries during the reforms of Diocletian and Constantine, and died under the onslaught of the barbarian tribes in the fifth century. The gravestone was laid in A.D. 476 when the last claimant to the Roman throne in the West was deposed, and that date was long taken to be the boundary between antique and modern society. This orthodoxy was rudely challenged by Henri Pirenne, who, in the 1920s, asserted that the Roman Empire survived in all its essentials until the coming of Islam destroyed the unity of the Mediterranean world.[1] At the other extreme is the view of Walbank — who finds the germs of the illness of antiquity already present in Athens in the fifth century B.C. — which suggests, in effect, that Rome began to die before her empire had been born. Between these extremes is the view held by others that the empire was really dead by A.D. 300, and it was only a ghostly apparition that the barbarians buried.

However little agreement there may be as to the time of Rome's demise, there is still less as to its cause. There are, perhaps, four applicable categories: death by accident, natural causes, murder, or suicide, and each is represented in these selections. The case for accidental death is made by J. B. Bury, who rejects all general causes. The theory of death from natural causes numbers Gibbon, Walbank, and de Ste. Croix among its adherents, although each sees the victim succumbing to a different disease. The case for suicide has many advocates. MacMullen, Rostovtzeff, Luttwak, and Ferrill believe that at some point

[1]See Alfred F. Havighurst, *The Pirenne Thesis* (1976), another title in the "Problems in European Civilization" series.

Rome embarked on a policy that ultimately led to her destruction, but each fixes on a different policy as responsible. Finally, there are those who believe that Rome fell by assassination. Baynes and Jones arrive by different paths at the conclusion that it was not a diseased cadaver that fell to the German invaders but a living organism.

Nor are these the only aspects of the problem. For some the idea of decline and fall is itself inappropriate. These scholars point out that, although they complained of hard times, the inhabitants of the Roman world at the time of its collapse knew nothing about it, and that their immediate descendants seemed unaware of any great difficulties involved in an analysis of Rome's decline and fall. The fact is that "the decline and fall of the Roman Empire" is a metaphor in which the empire is compared with an edifice; like all metaphors it conveys general impressions but not precise conceptions.

The Roman Empire was not a building, but a complex system of government administration presiding over a vast area containing a very heterogeneous group of peoples and modes of life. These were held together by certain common institutions and by the power and skill of the Roman state. What does it mean to speak of the decline and fall of a set of relationships? The difficulty of the question has led some historians to abandon the concept of decline and fall altogether, and to consider it rather in terms of disintegration and transformation. For them the Roman Empire never fell at all, but metamorphosed into something else. This is the theme of Part III. Peter Brown emphasizes the change in the geographic context of the world of late antiquity, and Ramsay MacMullen describes the change in its social character. Arther Ferrill, on the other hand, insists that Rome fell in the fifth century of the Christian era and that the event is one of the most important in human history.

The world of medieval Europe was radically different from that of the classical period — as different as the cathedral at Chartres is from the Parthenon in Athens or the Pantheon in Rome. It is, therefore, proper to retain Gibbon's statement of the problem, for whenever and however the Roman world fell or was transformed into something different, there was a point at which it no longer stood. From the variety and multiplicity of the solutions offered, it may appear that no progress is possible in the search for understanding. In fact, the situation is not so bad as that, for most students of the problem first clear the field for their own interpretations by pointing out the shortcomings of other opinions. Thus, an important part of the selections presented herein is the careful criticism they offer of previous ideas. In this way, the less persuasive or altogether baseless theories may be weeded out and discarded. Still, there is no consensus, and it is safe to guess that future historians will bring to the problem of Rome's collapse new ideas, deriving in part from the experience of their own age, while at the same time they seek to shed light on their own problems, which will have emanated, to a greater or lesser extent, from the circumstances of Rome's fall.

Variety of Opinion

The truth is that the success of the barbarians in penetrating and founding states in the western provinces cannot be explained by any general considerations. It is accounted for by the actual events and would be clearer if the story were known more fully. The gradual collapse of the Roman power in this section of the Empire was the consequence of a series of contingent events. No *general cause can be assigned that made it inevitable.*

J. B. Bury

The decline of Rome was the natural and inevitable effect of immoderate greatness. Prosperity ripened the principle of decay; the causes of destruction multiplied with the extent of conquest; and, as soon as time or accident had removed the artificial supports, the stupendous fabric yielded to the pressure of its own weight. The story of its ruin is simple and obvious; and instead of inquiring why the Roman Empire was destroyed, we should rather be surprised that it had subsisted so long.

Edward Gibbon

[The destructive tendencies of the Roman Empire arose] from the premises upon which classical civilization arose, namely an absolutely low technique and, to compensate for this, the institution of slavery. Herein lies the real cause of the decline and fall of the Roman Empire.

F. W. Walbank

The main phenomenon which underlies the process of decline is the gradual absorption of the educated classes by the masses and the consequent simplification of all the functions of political, social, economic, and intellectual life, which we call the barbarization of the ancient world.

Michael I. Rostovtzeff

It was, I suggest, the combination of unlimited economic power and political power in the hands of the propertied class, their emperor, and his administration which ultimately brought about the disintegration of the Roman empire. . . . If I were to search for a metaphor to describe the great and growing concentration of wealth in the hands of the upper classes, I would not incline towards anything so innocent and so automatic as drainage. I should want to think in terms of something much more purposive and deliberate — perhaps the vampire bat.

G. E. M. de Ste. Croix

I have identified thirteen defects which, in my view, combined to reduce the Roman Empire to final paralysis. They display a unifying thread: the thread of disunity. *Each defect consists of a specific disunity which split the Empire wide apart, and thereby damaged the capacity of the Romans to meet external aggressions. Heaven forbid that we ourselves should have a monolithic society without any internal disunities at all, or any differences of character or opinion. But there can arrive a time when such differences become so irreconcilably violent that the entire structure of society is imperiled. That is what happened among the ancient Romans. And that is why Rome fell.*

Michael Grant

The purpose of this book is to show how energies both harmonious and hostile to the Roman order appeared in a given class at a given time. As the locus of these energies moved down the social scale in the course of the first four centuries of the Empire, so the enemies of the state were, to begin with, drawn from senatorial ranks and, in the end, from peasants and barbarians. The drift of directing power outward and downward from the Roman aristocracy is well known; its corollary is the simultaneous movement of anti-Establishment impulses in the same direction.

Ramsay MacMullen

It was the increasing pressure of the barbarians, concentrated on the weaker western half of the empire, that caused the collapse.

A. H. M. Jones

It was the pitiful poverty of Western Rome which crippled her in her effort to maintain that civil and military system which was the presupposition for the continued life of the ancient civilization.

N. H. Baynes

It is apparent that reductions made in the provincial forces that guarded the frontiers in order to strengthen the central field armies would always serve to provide political security for the imperial power, but they must inevitably have downgraded the day-to-day security of the common people. In the very late stages of imperial devolution in the West, it is not unusual to find the frontiers stripped wholesale of their remaining garrisons, to augment central field forces. . . . In such cases the frontier was seemingly left to be "defended" by barbarian alliances, which were hollow versions of the client relationships of the first century. Such alliances were rented, not bought; inducements could provide no security once the indispensable element of deterrence was gone.

Edward N. Luttwak

Rome's army had always been small, relative to the population of the Empire, because Roman training and discipline gave it an unparalleled advantage in tactically effective, close-order formation. By 451, to judge from the speech Attila gave to the Huns at the battle of Châlons, the feeble remnant of the once-proud legions still fought in the ancient formation, but apparently without the training and discipline. Without them, close order was worse than no order at all. Romans could be expected to huddle behind their screen of shields; Visigoths and Alans would do the fighting. As the western army became barbarized, it lost its tactical superiority, and Rome fell to the onrush of barbarism.

Arther Ferrill

As the Mediterranean receded, so a more ancient world came to light. Small things sometimes betray changes more faithfully, because unconsciously. Near Rome, a sculptor's yard of the fourth century still turned out statues, impeccably dressed in the old Roman toga (with a socket for detachable portrait-heads!), but the aristocrats who commissioned such works would, in fact, wear a costume which betrayed prolonged exposure to the "barbarians" of the non-Mediterranean world — a woollen shirt from the Danube, a cloak from northern Gaul, fastened at the shoulders by a filigree brooch from Germany, even guarding their health by "Saxon" trousers. Deeper still, at the very core of the Mediterranean, the tradition of Greek philosophy had found a way of opening itself to a different religious mood.

Such changes as these are the main themes of the evolution of the Late Antique world.

Peter Brown

Emperor Constantine (306–337). Constantine placed a colossal statue of himself, nearly forty feet high, in his monumental basilica near the Roman Forum. This huge face from that statue is characteristic of Constantine's autocratic rule. (Alinari/Art Resource)

PART

The Problem of Decline and Fall Stated

Michael I. Rostovtzeff

The Decay of Ancient Civilization

Michael I. Rostovtzeff, born in Kiev in 1870, was educated at the universities of Kiev and St. Petersburg. He was Professor of Latin and Roman History at St. Petersburg until the Communist revolution in 1918. He came to the United States in 1920 and took up a position at the University of Wisconsin. Five years later he was appointed Sterling Professor of Ancient History and Classical Archaeology at Yale, a position he held until his retirement. In 1935 he was president of the American Historical Association. Among his more outstanding contributions are *The Social and Economic History of the Hellenistic World*, and *A History of the Ancient World*.

Reprinted from *Social and Economic History of the Roman Empire* by M. I. Rostovtzeff, 2nd ed. rev. by P. M. Fraser, Vol. I. (1957) by permission of Oxford University Press.

Every reader of a volume devoted to the Roman Empire will expect the author to express his opinion on what is generally, since Gibbon, called the decline and fall of the Roman Empire, or rather of ancient civilization in general. I shall therefore briefly state my own view on this problem, after defining what I take the problem to be. The decline and fall of the Roman Empire, that is to say, of ancient civilization as a whole, has two aspects: the political, social, and economic on the one hand, and the intellectual and spiritual on the other. In the sphere of politics we witness a gradual barbarization of the Empire from within, especially in the West. The foreign, German, elements play the leading part both in the government and in the army, and settling-in masses displace the Roman population, which disappears from the fields. A related phenomenon, which indeed was a necessary consequence of this barbarization from within, was the gradual disintegration of the Western Roman Empire; the ruling classes in the former Roman provinces were replaced first by Germans and Sarmatians, and later by Germans alone, either through peaceful penetration or by conquest. In the East we observe a gradual orientalization of the Byzantine Empire, which leads ultimately to the establishment, on the ruins of the Roman Empire, of strong half-Oriental and purely Oriental states, the Caliphate of Arabia, and the Persian and Turkish empires. From the social and economic point of view, we mean by decline the gradual relapse of the ancient world to very primitive forms of economic life, into an almost pure "house-economy." The cities, which had created and sustained the higher forms of economic life, gradually decayed, and the majority of them practically disappeared from the face of the earth. A few, especially those that had been great centers of commerce and industry, still lingered on. The complicated and refined social system of the ancient Empire follows the same downward path and becomes reduced to its primitive elements: the king, his court and retinue, the big feudal landowners, the clergy, the mass of rural serfs, and small groups of artisans and merchants. Such is the political, social, and economic aspect of the problem. However, we must not generalize too much. The Byzantine Empire cannot be put on a level with the states of Western Europe or with the new Slavonic formations. But one thing is certain: on the ruins of the uniform economic life of the cities there began everywhere a special, locally differentiated, evolution.

From the intellectual and spiritual point of view the main phenomenon is the decline of ancient civilization, of the city-civilization of the Greco-Roman world. The Oriental civilizations were more stable: blended with some elements of the Greek city-civilization, they persisted and even witnessed a brilliant revival in the Caliphate of Arabia and in Persia, not to speak of India and China. Here again there are two aspects of the evolution. The first is the exhaustion of the creative forces of Greek civilization in the domains where its great triumphs had been achieved, in the exact sciences, in technique, in literature and art. The decline began as early as the second century B.C. There followed a temporary revival of creative forces in the cities of Italy, and later in those of the Eastern and Western provinces of the Empire. The progressive movement stopped almost completely in the second century A.D. and, after a period of stagnation, a steady and rapid decline set in again. Parallel to it, we notice a progressive weakening of the assimilative forces of Greco-Roman civilization. The cities no longer absorb — that is to say, no longer hellenize or romanize — the masses of the country population. The reverse is the case. The barbarism of the country begins to engulf the city population. Only small islands of civilized life are left, the senatorial aristocracy of the late Empire and the clergy; but both, save for a section of the clergy, are gradually swallowed up by the advancing tide of barbarism.

Another aspect of the same phenomenon is the development of a new mentality among the masses of the population. It was the mentality of the lower classes, based exclusively on religion and not only indifferent but hostile to the intellectual achievements of the higher classes. This new attitude of mind gradually dominated the upper classes, or at least the larger part of them. It is revealed by the spread among them of the various mystic religions, partly Oriental, partly Greek. The climax was reached in the triumph of Christianity. In this field the creative power of the ancient world was still alive, as is shown by such momentous achievements as the creation of the Christian church, the adaptation of Christian theology to the mental level of the higher classes, the creation of a powerful Christian literature and of a new Christian art. The new intellectual efforts aimed chiefly at influencing the mass of the population and therefore represented a lowering of the high standards of city-civilization, at least from the point of view of literary forms.

We may say, then, that there is one prominent feature in the development of the ancient world during the imperial age, alike in the political, social, and economic and in the intellectual field. It is a gradual absorption of the higher classes by the lower, accompanied by a gradual leveling down of standards. This leveling was accomplished in many ways. There was a slow penetration of the lower classes into the higher, which were unable to assimilate the new elements. There were violent outbreaks of civil strife: the lead was taken by the Greek cities, and there followed the civil war of the first century B.C. which involved the whole civilized world. In these struggles the upper classes and the city-civilization remained victorious on the whole. Two centuries later, a new outbreak of civil war ended in the victory of the lower classes and dealt a mortal blow to the Greco-Roman civilization of the cities. Finally, that civilization was completely engulfed by the inflow of barbarous elements from outside, partly by penetration, partly by conquest, and in its dying condition it was unable to assimilate even a small part of them.

The main problem, therefore, which we have to solve is this. Why was the city-civilization of Greece and Italy unable to assimilate the masses, why did it remain a civilization of the *élite*, why was it incapable of creating conditions which should secure for the ancient world a continuous, uninterrupted movement along the same path of urban civilization? In other words: Why had modern civilization to be built up laboriously as something new on the ruins of the old, instead of being a direct continuation of it?

F. W. Walbank

The Nature of the Problem

Frank William Walbank, Rathbone Professor of Ancient History and Classical Archaeology at the University of Liverpool, was born in 1909 and educated at Cambridge. He is the author of biographies of Aratus of Sicyon and Philip V of Macedon. Volumes I and II of his major work, *A Historical Commentary on Polybius*, were published in 1957 and 1967.

[After briefly summarizing the views of the decline of the Roman Empire held by such men as Petrarch, Machiavelli, Voltaire, and Gibbon, the author continues:]

These examples may serve to illustrate the peculiarly topical shape which the problem of the decline of Rome invariably assumed. From it each age in turn has tried to formulate its own conception of progress and decadence. What, men have asked repeatedly, is the criterion by which we determine the point at which a society begins to decay? What is the yardstick by which we are to measure progress? And what are the symptoms and causes of decadence? The variety of answers given to these questions is calculated to depress the inquiring reader. When so many representative thinkers can find so many and such various explanations, according to the age in which they live, is there any hope, he will ask, of an answer that can claim more than purely relative validity?

The problem of progress and decadence (if we may so term it) has indeed evoked a variety of solutions. At some periods, as we have seen — particularly during the Renaissance — the question is broached in terms of political issues; society goes forward or back according to how questions of popular liberty, the power of the state, the existence of

Reprinted by permission of Lawrence & Wishart Ltd., from F. W. Walbank, *The Decline of the Roman Empire in the West* (New York, 1953), pp. 3–7.

tensions within its own structure are settled. At other times the moral note is struck: decay appears as a decline in ethical standards, whether through the removal of salutary threats from without or through the incursion of luxury. Both these approaches are essentially "naturalistic" in that they attempt to deduce the forms of progress and decadence from man's own acts, moral or political; and they stand in contrast to what has, on the whole, been the more usual attitude to the problem — the religious or mystical approach.

By some the rise and fall of empires have been interpreted (as among the early Christians) in prophetic terms, so as to conform with an apocalyptic picture of "four world kingdoms" or "six world ages." Another view treats history as a succession of civilizations, each reproducing the growth and decline of a living organism, in accordance with a kind of biological law. Or again civilizations are regarded as developing in cycles, one following straight after and repeating another, so that history is virtually a revolving wheel. Propounded originally by Plato (*c.* 427-347 B.C.) this cyclical theory found favor with Polybius (*c.* 200-117 B.C.), the Greek historian of Rome's rise to power, who thought it explained certain signs of decadence which his keen eye had detected at the height of Roman success. Taken over from Polybius by Machiavelli, this cyclical theory was adapted by G. B. Vico in the eighteenth century, and has its disciples in our own day. Similarly, the biological conception has become part of the common currency of historical writing. "The vast fabric," a modern scholar and statesman has written of the Roman Empire,[1] "succumbed in time, as all human institutions do, to the law of decay." All generalizations of this kind are at the root mystical.

These various answers seem largely to depend on where one starts. And perhaps the most satisfactory starting-point is the body which itself progresses and decays. For progress and decay are functions, not of isolated individuals, but of men and women knit together in society. It is society which goes forward or backward; and civilization is essentially a quality of social man. Aristotle made this point when he defined the state as originating in the bare needs of life and continuing in existence for the sake of the good life (*Politics* 1.2.8, 1252*b*). Evidently,

[1] H. H. Asquith, *The Legacy of Rome*, ed. Cyril Bailey (Oxford, 1923), p. 1.

therefore, when we say a society is in decay, we refer to something having gone wrong within its structure, or in the relationship between the various groups which compose it. The problem of decadence, like the problem of progress, is at the root a problem of man in society.

Now it is precisely this fact which gives ground for hoping that today it may be possible to say something new, and something of absolute validity upon the problem of the decline of the Roman Empire. For it is in our knowledge of the social man of antiquity that there has been the greatest revolution in the classical studies of the last sixty years.

In the past, ancient history was inevitably subjected to a double distortion. Our knowledge of the past could come in the main only from the writers of the past. In the last resort historians were dependent on their literary sources, and had to accept, roughly speaking, the world these drew. In addition there was the bias which the historian himself invariably imports into what he writes, rendered the more dangerous because he could let his fancy play, with no external control beyond his literary sources. Today the picture is quite different. For over fifty years classical scholars of many nationalities have been busy digging, classifying and interpreting material which was never meant for the historian's eye, and is for that reason invaluable evidence about the age which produced it. Buried towns like Pompeii and Herculaneum, with their houses, shops and equipment; inscriptions set up to embody some government decree in Athens or Ephesus, or to record some financial transaction on Delos, or the manumission of a slave at Delphi; the dedication of countless soldiers to their favorite deity, Mithras or perhaps some purely local goddess, like Coventina at Carrawburgh in Northumberland; papyrus fragments of household accounts and the libraries of great houses, salvaged from the sand of Oxyrhyncus and the mummy-cases of Roman Egypt; together with a scientific rereading and reinterpreting of the ancient texts in the light of this new knowledge, all these have opened up new vistas for the historian of social and economic life.

Now for the first time it is possible to turn a microscope on the ancient world. From the consideration of thousands of separate instances, general trends have been deduced, statistical laws have been established. We can now see beyond the individual to the life of society as a whole; and with that change in perspective we are able to determine directions where the literary sources showed us none. This does not, of course, mean that the classical authors may now be neglected. On the contrary they have become doubly valuable, for the light they throw on (and receive from) the new evidence. For consecutive history we still depend on the literary sources with their personal details; but the new discoveries give them a new dimension, particularly in all that concerns social or "statistical" man. The bias of our sources has thus largely been overcome; and though the presuppositions of the historian himself survive as an indissoluble residuum, the scientific, "indisputable" character of the new evidence frequently controls the answer, like the materials of a laboratory experiment. Thus for the first time in history it has become possible to analyze the course of decay in the Roman world with a high degree of objectivity.

A. H. M. Jones

East and West

Arnold Hugh Martin Jones was born in 1904 and died in 1970. He was educated at Oxford where he later held a lectureship. Subsequently he held the position of Professor of Ancient History at University College, London, and at Cambridge University. The author of many works on ancient Greek as well as Roman history, his main interest was in economic and social history and in the history of institutions. The excerpts in this volume represent the conclusions he reached after a lifetime of consideration of Roman imperial history.

The sack of Rome by Alaric in 410 caused a tremendous shock to Christians and pagans alike. Jerome, when he heard the news in Bethlehem, declared: "When the brightest light on the whole earth was extinguished, when the Roman empire was deprived of its head, when, to

From *The Later Roman Empire, 284-602* A.D. by A. H. M. Jones (3 vols.; Basil Blackwell, 1964). Reprinted by permission of the publisher.

speak more correctly, the whole world perished in one city, then 'I was dumb with silence. I held my peace, even from good, and my sorrow was stirred.'" Only a decade earlier Claudian had written: "There will never be an end to the power of Rome," and Ammianus had believed that "as long as there are men Rome will be victorious and will increase with lofty growth." The fall of Rome spelled the fall of the empire; it even meant the end of the world. A century before Lactantius had written: "The fall and ruin of the world will soon take place, but it seems that nothing of the kind is to be feared as long as the city of Rome stands intact. But when the capital of the world has fallen . . . who can doubt that the end will have come for the affairs of men and for the whole world? It is that city which sustains all things."

To pagans the explanation of the catastrophe was only too obvious. The misfortunes of the empire had increased with the growth of Christianity. The final disaster had come only a few years after Theodosius the Great had closed the temples and banned the worship of the gods. It was plain that the ancient gods by whose favor Rome had climbed to universal power had withdrawn their protection and were chastising the faithless Romans who had abandoned their worship.

The Christians made several answers, none of them very convincing. Orosius in his *Historia contra Paganos* set out to prove that the history of Rome while she still worshipped the gods had been one uninterrupted series of disasters, and that with the barbarians in Spain and Gaul exterminating one another and vying to take service under the empire, things were now at last taking a turn for the better. This was too perverse to carry conviction to any reasonable man. Despite occasional misfortunes Rome had been victorious and had won a great empire under the old dispensation. Things did not get better, but went from bad to worse, and Salvian a generation later took a quite different line in his *de Gubernatione Dei*. The disasters of the empire, he argued, were the chastisement inflicted by God on the Romans for their sins, their loose sexual morals, their oppression of the poor, and their addiction to the games. By contrast, reviving the legend of the noble savage, he pictured the barbarians as perhaps uncouth but chaste, austere and righteous. The refugees whose homes had been plundered and burned, the free men who had been carried off and sold into slavery, the sacred virgins whom the Vandals had raped by the score, cannot have found Salvian's arguments very convincing.

Augustine in *The City of God* used both these arguments, but his main theme was different. It was true, he admitted, that in the *civitas terrena* pagan Rome had prospered and the history of the Christian empire had been calamitous. But what did the things of this world matter in comparison with the spiritual world, the *civitas Dei*? To the Christian earthly disasters were indifferent, they were even to be welcomed as sent by God to discipline and purify the faithful. This world was only a vale of tears, and true blessedness was to be found in the life of the spirit here on earth, and in all its fullness in the world to come.

In the eighteenth century the debate on the fall of the empire was resumed, and it has gone on ever since. Rationalists like Gibbon saw religion as a primary cause of its decline, but in a very different way from the pagan and Christian controversialists of the fifth century. Christianity in his view sapped the morale of the empire, deadened its intellectual life and by its embittered controversies undermined its unity. Other historians, according to the temper of their times, have emphasized the empire's military decline, its political or social weaknesses, or its economic decay.

All the historians who have discussed the decline and fall of the Roman Empire have been Westerners. Their eyes have been fixed on the collapse of Roman authority in the Western parts and the evolution of the medieval Western European world. They have tended to forget, or to brush aside, one very important fact, that the Roman Empire, though it may have declined, did not fall in the fifth century nor indeed for another thousand years. During the fifth century, while the Western parts were being parceled out into a group of barbarian kingdoms, the empire of the East stood its ground. In the sixth it counterattacked and reconquered Africa from the Vandals and Italy from the Ostrogoths, and part of Spain from the Visigoths. Before the end of the century, it is true, much of Italy and Spain had succumbed to renewed barbarian attacks, and in the seventh the onslaught of the Arabs robbed the empire of Syria, Egypt, and Africa, and the Slavs overran the Balkans. But in Asia Minor the empire lived on, and later, recovering its strength, reconquered much territory that it had lost in the dark days of the seventh century.

These facts are important, for they demonstrate that the empire did not, as some modern historians have suggested, totter into its grave from senile decay, impelled by a gentle push from the barbarians. Most of the internal weaknesses which these historians stress were common to both halves of the empire. The East was even more Christian than the West, its theological disputes far more embittered. The East, like the West, was administered by a corrupt and extortionate bureaucracy. The Eastern government strove as hard to enforce a rigid caste system, tying the *curiales* to their cities and the *coloni* to the soil. Land fell out of cultivation and was deserted in the East as well as in the West. It may be that some of these weaknesses were more accentuated in the West than in the East, but this is a question which needs investigation. It may be also that the initial strength of the Eastern empire in wealth and population was greater, and that it could afford more wastage; but this again must be demonstrated.

Double aureus of Diocletian ca. 284–305 A.D. This gold coin carries the picture of the emperor Diocletian. He put an end to the chaos of third century Rome and reorganized the Empire on a new and more solid basis. (Courtesy, Museum of Fine Arts, Boston)

The Causes

Natural Decline

J. B. Bury

Decline and Calamities of the Empire

John Bagnell Bury was born in Dublin in 1861 and was educated there at Trinity College. From 1902 until his death in 1927 he was Regius Professor of Modern History at Cambridge University. His textbook on the history of Greece remains a classic in its field, as does his *Ancient Greek Historians*. His edition of Gibbon is the best ever done. Bury's interest in the philosophy of history is demonstrated by two of his works, *The History of Freedom of Thought* and *The Idea of Progress*.

The explanations of the calamities of the Empire which have been hazarded by modern writers are of a different order from those which occurred to witnesses of the events, but they are not much more satisfying. The illustrious historian whose name will always be associated

From J. B. Bury, *History of the Later Roman Empire*, 395-565 (2 vols.; London, 1923), Vol. I, 308-13. Reprinted by permission of Macmillan & Company Ltd. (London).

with the "Decline" of the Roman Empire invoked "the principle of decay," a principle which has itself to be explained. Depopulation, the Christian religion, the fiscal system have all been assigned as causes of the Empire's decline in strength. If these or any of them were responsible for its dismemberment by the barbarians in the West, it may be asked how it was that in the East, where the same causes operated, the Empire survived much longer intact and united.

Consider depopulation. The depopulation of Italy was an important fact and it had far-reaching consequences. But it was a process which had probably reached its limit in the time of Augustus. There is no evidence that the Empire was less populous in the fourth and fifth centuries than in the first. The "sterility of the human harvest" in Italy and Greece affected the history of the Empire from its very beginning, but does not explain the collapse in the fifth century. The truth is that there are two distinct questions which have been confused. It is one thing to seek the causes which changed the Roman state from what it was in the best days of the Republic to what it had become in the age of Theodosius the Great — a change which from certain points of view may be called a "decline." It is quite another thing to ask why the state which could resist its enemies on many frontiers in the days of Diocletian and Constantine and Julian suddenly gave way in the days of Honorius. "Depopulation" may partly supply the answer to the first question, but it is not an answer to the second. Nor can the events which transferred the greater part of western Europe to German masters be accounted for by the numbers of the peoples who invaded it. The notion of vast hosts of warriors, numbered by hundreds of thousands, pouring over the frontiers, is, as we saw, perfectly untrue. The total number of one of the large East German nations probably seldom exceeded 100,000, and its army of fighting men can rarely have been more than from 20,000 to 30,000. They were not a deluge, overwhelming and irresistible, and the Empire had a well-organized military establishment at the end of the fourth century, fully sufficient in capable hands to beat them back. As a matter of fact, since the defeat at Hadrianople which was due to the blunders of Valens, no very important battle was won by German over Imperial forces during the whole course of the invasions.

It has often been alleged that Christianity in its political effects was a disintegrating force and tended to weaken the power of Rome to resist her enemies. It is difficult to see that it had any such tendency, so long as the Church itself was united. Theological heresies were indeed to prove a disintegrating force in the East in the seventh century, when differences in doctrine which had alienated the Christians in Egypt and Syria from the government of Constantinople facilitated the conquests of the Saracens. But, after the defeat of Arianism, there was no such vital or deep-reaching division in the West, and the effect of Christianity was to unite, not to sever, to check, rather than to emphasize, national or sectional feeling. In the political calculations of Constantine it was probably this idea of unity, as a counterpoise to the centrifugal tendencies which had been clearly revealed in the third century, that was the great recommendation of the religion which he raised to power. Nor is there the least reason to suppose that Christian teaching had the practical effect of making men less loyal to the Empire or less ready to defend it. The Christians were as pugnacious as the pagans. Some might read Augustine's *City of God* with edification, but probably very few interpreted its theory with such strict practical logic as to be indifferent to the safety of the Empire. Hardly the author himself, though this has been disputed.

It was not long after Alaric's capture of Rome that Volusian, a pagan senator of a distinguished family, whose mother was a Christian and a friend of Augustine, proposed the question whether the teaching of Christianity is not fatal to the welfare of a state, because a Christian smitten on one cheek would if he followed the precepts of the Gospel turn the other to the smiter. We have the letter in which Augustine answers the question and skillfully explains the text so as to render it consistent with common sense. And to show that warfare is not forbidden, another text is quoted in which soldiers who ask "What shall we do?" are bidden to "Do violence to no man, neither accuse any falsely, and be content with your wages." They are not told not to serve or fight. The bishop goes on to suggest that those who wage a just war are really acting *misericorditer*, in a spirit of mercy and kindness to their enemies, as it is to the true interests of their enemies that their vices should be corrected. Augustine's *misericorditer* laid down unintentionally a dangerous and hypocritical doctrine for the justification of war, the same principle which was used for justifying the Inquisition. But his definite statement that the Christian discipline does not condemn all wars was equivalent to saying that Christians were bound as much as pagans to defend Rome against the barbarians. And this was the general view. All the leading Churchmen of the fifth century were devoted to the Imperial idea, and when they worked for peace or compromise, as they often did, it was always when the cause of the barbarians was in the ascendant and resistance seemed hopeless.

The truth is that the success of the barbarians in penetrating and founding states in the western provinces cannot be explained by any general considerations. It is accounted for by the actual events and would be clearer if the story were known more fully. The gradual collapse of the Roman power in this section of the Empire was the consequence of *a series of contingent events*. No general causes can be assigned that made it inevitable.

The first contingency was the irruption of the Huns into Europe, an event resulting from causes which were quite independent of the weakness or strength of the Roman Empire. It drove the Visigoths into the Illyrian provinces, and the difficult situation was unhappily mismanaged. One Emperor was defeated and lost his life; it was his own fault. That disaster, which need not have occurred, was a second contingency. His successor allowed a whole federate nation to settle on provincial soil; he took the line of least resistance and established an unfortunate precedent. He did not foresee consequences which, if he had lived ten or twenty years longer, might not have ensued. His death was a third contingency. But the situation need have given no reason for grave alarm if the succession had passed to an Emperor like himself, or Valentinian I, or even Gratian. Such a man was not procreated by Theodosius and the government of the West was inherited by a feeble-minded boy. That was a fourth event, dependent on causes which had nothing to do with the condition of the Empire.

In themselves these events need not have led to disaster. If the guardian of Honorius and director of his government had been a man of Roman birth and tradition, who commanded the public confidence, a man such as Honorius himself was afterwards to find in Constantius and his successor in Aetius, all might have been tolerably well. But there was a point of weakness in the Imperial system, the practice of elevating Germans to the highest posts of command in the army. It had grown up under Valentinian I, Gratian, and Theodosius; it had led to the rebellion of Maximus, and had cost Valentinian II his life. The German in whom Theodosius reposed his confidence and who assumed the control of affairs on his death probably believed that he was serving Rome faithfully, but it was a singular misfortune that at a critical moment when the Empire had to be defended not only against Germans without but against a German nation which had penetrated inside, the responsibility should have devolved upon a German. Stilicho did not intend to be a traitor, but his policy was as calamitous as if he had planned deliberate treachery. For it meant civil war. The dissatisfaction of the Romans in the West was expressed in the rebellion of Constantine, the successor of Maximus, and if Stilicho had had his way the soldiers of Honorius and of Arcadius would have been killing one another for the possession of Illyricum. When he died the mischief was done; Goths had Italy at their mercy, Gaul and Spain were overrun by other peoples. His Roman successors could not undo the results of events which need never have happened.

The supremacy of a Stilicho was due to the fact that the defense of the Empire had come to depend on the enrollment of barbarians, in large numbers, in the army, and that it was necessary to render the service attractive to them by the prospect of power and wealth. This was, of course, a consequence of the decline in military spirit, and of depopulation, in the old civilized Mediterranean countries. The Germans in high command had been useful, but the dangers involved in the policy had been shown in the cases of Merobaudes and Arbogastes. Yet this policy need not have led to the dismemberment of the Empire, and but for that series of chances its western provinces would not have been converted, as and when they were, into German kingdoms. It may be said that a German penetration of western Europe must ultimately have come about. But even if that were certain, it might have happened in another way, at a later time, more gradually, and with less violence. The point of the present contention is that Rome's loss of her provinces in the fifth century was not an "inevitable effect of any of those features which have been rightly or wrongly described as causes or consequences of her general 'decline.'" The central fact that Rome could not dispense with the help of barbarians for her wars *(gentium barbararum auxilio indigemus)* may be held to be the cause of her calamities, but it was a weakness which might have continued to be far short of fatal but for the sequence of contingencies pointed out above.

Edward Gibbon

General Observations on the Fall of the Roman Empire in the West

Edward Gibbon was born in Putney, England in 1737. His great work, *Decline and Fall of the Roman Empire*, published between 1776 and 1788, brought him fame and membership in the illustrious circle of Dr. Johnson. It is one of the great classics of historical literature and one of the best products of the thought of the eighteenth-century Enlightenment.

The Greeks, after their country had been reduced into a province, imputed the triumphs of Rome, not to the merit, but to the *Fortune* of the republic. The inconstant goddess, who so blindly distributes and resumes her favors, had *now* consented (such was the language of envious flattery) to resign her wings, to descend from her globe, and to fix her firm and immutable throne on the banks of the Tiber. A wiser Greek, who has composed, with a philosophic spirit, the memorable history of his own times, deprived his countrymen of this vain and delusive comfort by opening to their view the deep foundations of the greatness of Rome. The fidelity of the citizens to each other, and to the state, was confirmed by the habits of education and the prejudices of religion. Honor, as well as virtue, was the principle of the republic; the ambitious citizens labored to deserve the solemn glories of a triumph; and the ardor of the Roman youth was kindled into active emulation, as often as they beheld the domestic images of their ancestors. The temperate struggles of the patricians and plebeians had finally established the firm and equal balance of the constitution; which united the freedom of popular assemblies with the authority and wisdom of a

From Edward Gibbon, *Decline and Fall of the Roman Empire* (London, 1901), Vol. IV, pp. 160–63.

senate and the executive powers of a regal magistrate. When the consul displayed the standard of the republic, each citizen bound himself, by the obligation of an oath, to draw his sword in the cause of his country, till he had discharged the sacred duty by a military service of ten years. This wise institution continually poured into the field the rising generations of freemen and soldiers; and their numbers were reinforced by the warlike and populous states of Italy, who, after a brave resistance, had yielded to the valor, and embraced the alliance, of the Romans. The sage historian, who excited the virtue of the younger Scipio and beheld the ruin of Carthage, has accurately described their military system; their levies, arms, exercises, subordination, marches, encampments; and the invincible legion, superior in active strength to the Macedonian phalanx of Philip and Alexander. From these institutions of peace and war, Polybius has deduced the spirit and success of a people incapable of fear and impatient of repose. The ambitious design of conquest, which might have been defeated by the seasonable conspiracy of mankind, was attempted and achieved; and the perpetual violation of justice was maintained by the political virtues of prudence and courage. The arms of the republic, sometimes vanquished in battle, always victorious in war, advanced with rapid steps to the Euphrates, the Danube, the Rhine, and the Ocean; and the images of gold, or silver, or brass, that might serve to represent the nations and their kings, were successively broken by the *iron* monarchy of Rome.

The rise of a city, which swelled into an empire, may deserve, as a singular prodigy, the reflection of a philosophic mind. But the decline of Rome was the natural and inevitable effect of immoderate greatness. Prosperity ripened the principle of decay; the causes of destruction multiplied with the extent of conquest; and, as soon as time or accident had removed the artificial supports, the stupendous fabric yielded to the pressure of its own weight. The story of its ruin is simple and obvious; and, instead of inquiring why the Roman empire was destroyed, we should rather be surprised that it had subsisted so long. The victorious legions, who, in distant wars, acquired the vices of strangers and mercenaries, first oppressed the freedom of the republic, and afterwards violated the majesty of the purple. The emperors, anxious for their personal safety and the public peace, were reduced to the base expedient of corrupting the discipline which rendered them alike formidable to their sovereign and to the enemy; the vigor of the military government was relaxed, and finally dissolved, by the partial institutions of Constantine; and the Roman world was overwhelmed by a deluge of Barbarians.

The decay of Rome has been frequently ascribed to the translation of the seat of empire; but this history has already shown that the powers of government were *divided* rather than *removed*. The throne of Constantinople was erected in the East; while the West was still possessed by a series of emperors who held their residence in Italy and claimed their equal inheritance of the legions and provinces. This dangerous novelty impaired the strength, and fomented the vices, of a double reign; the instruments of an oppressive and arbitrary system were multiplied; and a vain emulation of luxury, not of merit, was introduced and supported between the degenerate successors of Theodosius. Extreme distress, which unites the virtue of a free people, embitters the factions of a declining monarchy. The hostile favorites of Arcadius and Honorius betrayed the republic to its common enemies; and the Byzantine court beheld with indifference, perhaps with pleasure, the disgrace of Rome, the misfortunes of Italy, and the loss of the West. Under the succeeding reigns, the alliance of the two empires was restored; but the aid of the Oriental Romans was tardy, doubtful, and ineffectual; and the national schism of the Greeks and Latins was enlarged by the perpetual difference of language and manners, of interest, and even of religion. Yet the salutary event approved in some measure the judgment of Constantine. During a long period of decay, his impregnable city repelled the victorious armies of Barbarians, protected the wealth of Asia, and commanded, both in peace and war, the important straits which connect the Euxine and Mediterranean seas. The foundation of Constantinople more essentially contributed to the preservation of the East than to the ruin of the West.

As the happiness of a *future* life is the great object of religion, we may hear, without surprise or scandal, that the introduction, or at least the abuse, of Christianity had some influence on the decline and fall of the Roman Empire. The clergy successfully preached the doctrines of patience and pusillanimity; the active virtues of society were discouraged; and the last remains of the military spirit were buried in the cloister; a large portion of public and private wealth was consecrated to the specious demands of charity and devotion; and the soldiers' pay was lavished on the useless multitudes of both sexes, who could only plead the merits of abstinence and chastity. Faith, zeal, curiosity, and the more earthly passions of malice and ambition kindled the flame of theological discord; the church, and even the state, were distracted by religious factions, whose conflicts were sometimes bloody, and always implacable; the attention of the emperors was diverted from camps to synods; the Roman world was oppressed by a new species of tyranny; and the persecuted sects became the secret enemies of their country. Yet party spirit, however pernicious or absurd, is a principle of union as well as of dissension. The bishops, from eighteen hundred pulpits, inculcated the duty of passive obedience to a lawful and orthodox sovereign; their frequent assemblies, and perpetual correspondence, maintained the communion of distant churches; and the benevolent temper of the gospel was strengthened, though confined, by the spiritual alliance of the Catholics. The sacred indolence of the monks was devoutly embraced by a servile and effeminate age; but, if superstition had not afforded a decent retreat, the same vices would have tempted the unworthy Romans to desert, from baser motives, the standard of the republic. Religious precepts are easily obeyed, which indulge and sanctify the natural inclinations of their votaries; but the pure and genuine influence of Christianity may be traced in its beneficial, though imperfect, effects on the Barbarian proselytes of the North. If the decline of the Roman Empire was hastened by the conversion of Constantine, his victorious religion broke the violence of the fall, and mollified the ferocious temper of the conquerors.

Social Analyses

Michael I. Rostovtzeff

The Empire During the Anarchy

Incomplete as it is, the picture which we have drawn shows very clearly the chaos and misery that reigned throughout the Roman Empire in the third century and especially in the second half of it. We have

Reprinted from *Social and Economic History of the Roman Empire* by M. I. Rostovtzeff, 2nd ed. rev. by P. M. Fraser, Vol. I. (1957) by permission of Oxford University Press.

endeavored to show how the Empire gradually reached this pitiful state. It was due to a combination of constant civil war and fierce attacks by external foes. The situation was aggravated by the policy of terror and compulsion which the government adopted towards the population, using the army as its instrument. The key to the situation lies, therefore, in the civil strife which provoked and made possible the onslaughts of neighboring enemies, weakened the Empire's powers of resistance, and forced the emperors, in dealing with the population, to have constant recourse to methods of terror and compulsion, which gradually developed into a more or less logically organized system of administration. In the policy of the emperors we failed to discover any systematic plan. It was a gradual yielding to the aspirations of the army and to the necessity of maintaining the existence of the Empire and preserving its unity. Most of the emperors of this troubled period were not ambitious men who were ready to sacrifice the interests of the community to their personal aspirations: they did not seek power for the sake of power. The best of them were forced to assume power, and they did it partly from a natural sense of self-preservation, partly as a conscious sacrifice of their own lives to the noble task of maintaining and safeguarding the Empire. If the state was transformed by the emperors on the lines described above, on the lines of a general leveling, by destroying the part played in the life of the Empire by the privileged and educated classes, by subjecting the people to a cruel and foolish system of administration based on terror and compulsion, and by creating a new aristocracy which sprang up from the rank and file of the army, and if this policy gradually produced a slave state with a small ruling minority headed by an autocratic monarch, who was commander of an army of mercenaries and of a militia compulsorily levied, it was not because such was the ideal of the emperors but because it was the easiest way of keeping the state going and preventing a final breakdown. But this goal could be achieved only if the army provided the necessary support: and the emperors clearly believed they could get its help by the policy they pursued.

If it was not the ambition of the emperors that drew the state ever deeper into the gulf of ruin, and threatened to destroy the very foundations of the Empire, what was the immanent cause which induced the army constantly to change the emperors, to slay those whom they had just proclaimed, and to fight their brothers with a fury that hardly finds a parallel in the history of mankind? Was it a "mass psychosis" that seized the soldiers and drove them forward on the path of destruction? Would it not be strange that such a mental disease should last for at least half a century? The usual explanation given by modern scholars suggests that the violent convulsions of the third century were the accompaniment of the natural and necessary transformation of the Roman state into an absolute monarchy. The crisis (it is said) was a political one; it was created by the endeavor of the emperors to eliminate the senate politically and to transform the Augustan diarchy into a pure monarchy; in striving towards this goal the emperors leaned on the army, corrupted it, and provoked the state of anarchy, which formed a transitional phase that led to the establishment of the Oriental despotism of the fourth century. We have endeavored to show that such an explanation does not stand the test of facts. The senate, as such, had no political importance whatsoever in the time of the enlightened monarchy. Its social prestige was high, for it represented the educated and propertied classes of the Empire, but its direct political participation in state affairs was very small. In order to establish the autocratic system of government there was not the slightest necessity to pass through a period of destruction and anarchy. Monarchy was established in actual fact by the Antonines without shedding a drop of blood. The real fight was not between the emperor and the senate.

The theory that a bloody struggle developed in the third century between the emperors and the senate must therefore be rejected as not fitting the facts. Certainly, the transformation of the principate into a military monarchy did not agree with the wishes of the senate, but that body had no political force to oppose to the emperors. Recognizing this fact, some leading modern scholars have attempted to explain the crisis in another way, but still in terms of political causes; on the assumption that the crisis of the third century arose not so much from the active opposition of the senate as from the relations between the emperors and the army. The new army of the second part of the third century was no longer the army of Roman citizens recruited from Italy and the romanized provinces; the elements of which it was composed were provinces of little or no romanization and warlike tribes recruited beyond its frontiers. No sooner had this army recognized its own power at the end of the Antonine age, than it was corrupted by the emperors with gifts and flattery, and familiarized with bribery; it felt itself master of the state and gave orders to the emperors. The conditions imposed by it were partly of a material, and partly, up to a certain point, of a political, nature: for example, that the privileges enjoyed by the ruling classes should be extended to the army. As the emperors had not succeeded in giving their power a juridical or religious basis which was sufficiently clear to convince the masses and the army without delay, it became increasingly clear that they governed only by the grace of the soldiers; each body of troops chose its own emperor and regarded him as the instrument for the satisfaction of its wishes.

This theory, which I hope I have summarized exactly, is undoubtedly nearer the truth and coincides in the main with the views set forth in this book [*Social and Economic History of the Roman Empire*]. I have shown how the Roman emperors tried hard to find a legal basis for their power. Emperors like Vespasian and, even more, Domitian saw clearly that the dynastic principle of hereditary succession, founded upon the Oriental conception of the divine nature of imperial power, and therefore upon the apotheosis of the living emperor, was much more intelligible to the masses than the subtle and complex theory of the principate as formulated by Augustus and applied by the majority of his successors, particularly the Antonines. Yet the simplification proposed by Domitian could not be accepted by the leading classes of the Roman Empire, since it implied the complete negation of the idea of liberty, which they cherished so dearly. These classes fought against the transformation of the principate into an unconcealed monarchy, and in their tenacious struggle they had, if not as an ally, at least not as an enemy, the army composed of citizens who held to a great extent the same opinions as themselves. The result was a compromise between the imperial power on one side, and the educated classes and the senate which represented them, on the other. This compromise was effected by the Antonines. When, at the end of the second century A.D., the barbarization of the army was complete, that body was no longer able to understand the delicate theory of the principate. It was instead prepared to accept the hereditary monarchy established by Septimius Severus, and the emperor, with the army's help, was able to suppress without difficulty the opposition aroused by his action. So far I am in the fullest agreement with the theory described above.

But at this point difficulties begin. Why did the dynasty of the Severi not last, after it had been established, and accepted willingly by the army and unwillingly by the educated classes? How are we to explain the fact that the soldiers murdered Severus Alexander, and later even killed and betrayed the emperors they had themselves elected, thereby creating that political chaos which exposed the Empire to the greatest dangers? The continuous upheavals must have had a deeper cause than the struggle for the hereditary monarchy of divine right. This goal had been reached from the first moment; why did the struggle continue for another fifty years?

Perhaps the wisest course would be to be satisfied with this partial explanation, in the company of the majority of scholars. Our evidence is scanty, and the most comfortable way is always that of *non liquet* and *ignoramus*. In the first edition of this work I dared to offer a theory which is to some extent supported by our inadequate evidence, and which, if it proved acceptable, would enable us to understand the nature of the crisis of the Roman Empire. The five pages devoted to this explanation attracted the attention of the majority of my critics, and much has been written against my "theory," though without a single fact being adduced against it. The chief argument invoked against my "theory" is that the trend of my thoughts was influenced by events in modern Russia. Without entering upon an argument on this topic, I see no reason to abandon my previous explanation simply because I may, or may not, have been led to it by the study of similar events in later history. It still satisfies me and agrees with the facts insofar as I know them.

In my opinion, when the political struggle which had been fought around the hereditary monarchy between the emperors, supported by the army, and the upper classes, came to an end, the same struggle was repeated in a different form. Now, no political aim was at stake: the issue between the army and the educated classes was the leadership of the state. The emperors were not always on the side of the army; many of them tried to preserve the system of government which the enlightened monarchy had based upon the upper classes. These efforts were, however, fruitless, since all concessions made by the emperors, any act which might mean a return to the conditions of the Antonine age, met the half-unconscious resistance of the army. In addition, the *bourgeoisie* was no longer able to give the emperors effective aid.

Such was the real meaning of the civil war of the third century. The army fought the privileged classes, and did not cease fighting until these classes had lost all their social prestige and lay powerless and prostrate under the feet of the half-barbarian soldiery. Can we, however, say that the soldiery fought out this fight for its own sake, with the definite plan of creating a sort of tyranny or dictatorship of the army over the rest of the population? There is not the slightest evidence in support of such a view. An elemental upheaval was taking place and developing. Its final goal may be comprehensible to us, but was not understood even by contemporaries and still less by the actors in the terrible tragedy. The driving forces were envy and hatred, and those who sought to destroy the rule of the bourgeois class had no positive program. The constructive work was gradually done by the emperors, who built on the ruins of a destroyed social order as well, or as badly, as it could be done and not in the least in the spirit of destroyers. The old privileged class was replaced by another, and the masses, far from being better off than they had been before, became much poorer and much more miserable. The only difference was that the ranks of the sufferers were swelled, and that the ancient civilized condition of the Empire had vanished forever.

If the army acted as the destroyer of the existing social order, it was not because as an army it hated that order. The position of the army was not bad even from the social point of view, since it was the natural source of recruits for the municipal *bourgeoisie*. It acted as a powerful destructive and leveling agent because it represented, at the end of the second century and during the third, those large masses of the population that had little share in the brilliant civilized life of the Empire. We have shown that the army of M. Aurelius and of Commodus was almost wholly an army of peasants, a class excluded from the advantages of urban civilization, and that this rural class formed the majority of the population of the Empire. Some of these peasants were small landowners, some were tenants or serfs of the great landlords or of the state; as a mass they were the subjects, while the members of the city aristocracy were the rulers; they formed the class of *humiliores* as contrasted with the *honestiores* of the towns, the class of *dediticii* as compared with the burgesses of the cities. In short, they were a special caste separated by a deep gulf from the privileged classes, a caste whose duty it was to support the high civilization of the cities by their toil and work, by their taxes and rents. The endeavors of the enlightened monarchy and of the Severi to raise this class, to elevate it into a village *bourgeoisie*, to assimilate as large a portion of it as possible to the privileged classes, and to treat the rest as well as possible, awakened in the minds of the *humiliores* the consciousness of their humble position and strengthened their allegiance to the emperors, but they failed to achieve their main aim. In truth, the power of the enlightened monarchy was based on the city *bourgeoisie*, and it was not the aim of the *bourgeoisie* to enlarge their ranks indefinitely and to share their privileges with large numbers of newcomers.

The result was that the dull submissiveness which had for centuries been the typical mood of the *humiliores* was gradually transformed into a sharp feeling of hatred and envy towards the privileged classes. These feelings were naturally reflected in the rank and file of the army, which now consisted exclusively of peasants. When, after the usurpation of Septimius, the army became gradually aware of its power and influence with the emperors, and when the emperors of his dynasty repeatedly emphasized their allegiance to it and their sympathy with the peasants, and treated the city *bourgeoisie* harshly, it gradually yielded to its feelings and began to exert a half-conscious pressure on the emperors, reacting violently against the concessions made by some of them to the hated class. The *bourgeoisie* attempted to assert its influence and to save its privileges, and the result was open war from time to time and a ruthless extermination of the privileged class. Violent outbreaks took place after the reign of Alexander, whose ideals were those of the enlightened monarchy, and more especially after the short period of restoration which followed the reaction of Maximinus. It was this restoration that was ultimately responsible for the dreadful experiences of the reign of Gallienus; and the policy consequently adopted by that emperor and most of his successors finally set aside the plan of restoring the rule of the cities, and met the wishes of the peasant army. This policy, although it was a policy of despair, at least saved the fabric of the Empire. The victory of the peasants over the city *bourgeoisie* was thus complete, and the period of the domination of city over country seemed to have ended. A new state based on a new foundation was built up by the successors of Gallienus, with only occasional reversions to the ideals of the enlightened monarchy.

It is, of course, not easy to prove our thesis that the antagonism between the city and the country was the main driving force of the social revolution of the third century. But the reader will recollect the picture we have drawn of Maximinus's policy, of his extermination of the city *bourgeoisie*, of the support given him by the African army of peasants against the city landowners; and he will bear in mind the violent outbreaks of military anarchy after the reign of Pupienus and Balbinus, of Gordian III, and of Philip. Many other facts testify to the same antagonism between country and city. It is remarkable how easily the soldiers could be induced to pillage and murder in the cities of the Roman Empire. We have already spoken of the destruction of Lyons by the soldiery after the victory of Septimius over Albinus, of the Alexandrian massacre of Caracalla, of the demand of the soldiers of Elagabal to loot the city of Antioch. We have alluded to the repeated outbreaks of civil war between the population of Rome and the soldiers. The fate of Byzantium, pillaged by its own garrison in the time of Gallienus, is typical. Still more characteristic of the mood both of the peasants and of the soldiers is the destruction of Augustodunum (Autun) in the time of Tetricus and Claudius in A.D. 269. When the city recognized Claudius, Tetricus sent a detachment of his army against the "rebels." It was joined by gangs of robbers and peasants. They cut off the water supply and finally took the flourishing city and destroyed it so utterly that it never revived. The two greatest creations of the period of urbanization in Gaul — Lyons and Autun — were thus laid in ruins by enraged soldiers and peasants. One of the richest cities of Asia Minor, Tyana, was in danger of suffering the same fate in the time of Aurelian. It was saved by the emperor, and the words he used to persuade the soldiers not to destroy it are interesting: "We are carrying on war to free these cities; if we are to pillage them, they will trust us no more. Let us seek the spoil of the barbarians and spare these men as our own people." It was evidently not easy to convince the soldiers that the cities of the Empire were not their chief enemies. The attitude of the soldiers towards them was like that of the plundering Goths, as described by Petrus Patricius. His words certainly expressed the feelings of many Roman soldiers. "The Scythians jeered at those who were shut up in the cities, saying, They live a life not of men but of birds sitting in their nests aloft; they leave the earth which nourishes them and choose barren cities; they put their trust in lifeless things rather than in themselves."

We have frequently noted also the close relations existing between the peasants and the soldiers. It was through soldiers that the peasants forwarded their petitions to the emperor in the time of Commodus and Septimius as well as in that of Philip and Gordian. In fact, most of the soldiers had no knowledge or understanding of the cities, but they kept up their relations with their native villages, and the villagers regarded their soldiers as their natural patrons and protectors, and looked on the emperor as their emperor and not as the emperor of the cities. . . . We described the important part played during the third century by soldiers and ex-soldiers in the life of the villages of the Balkan peninsula and Syria, the lands of free peasant *possessores*, as contrasted with the lands of tenants or *coloni*, and we pointed out that they formed the real aristocracy of the villages and served as intermediaries between the village and the administrative authorities. We showed how large was the infiltration of former soldiers into the country parts of Africa in the same century; and in describing the conditions of Egypt during that period we repeatedly drew attention to the large part played in the economic life of the land by active and retired soldiers. All this serves to show that the ties between the villages and the army were never broken, and that it was natural that the army should share the aspirations of the villages and regard the dwellers in the cities as aliens and enemies.

Despite the changed conditions at the end of the fourth century, the relations between the army and the villages remained exactly as they had been in the third. The cities still existed, and the municipal aristocracy was still used by the government to collect the taxes and exact compulsory work from the inhabitants of the villages. It was no wonder that, even after the cities almost completely lost their political and social influence, the feelings of the peasants towards them did not change. For the villages the cities were still the oppressors and exploiters. Occasionally such feelings are expressed by writers of the fourth century, both Western (chiefly African) and Eastern, especially the latter. Our information is unusually good for Syria, and particularly for the neighborhood of Antioch, thanks to Libanius and John Chrysostom. One of the leading themes which we find in both writers is the antagonism between city and country. In this constant strife the government had no definite policy, but the soldiers sided with the peasants against the great men from the cities. The sympathies of the soldiers are sufficiently shown by the famous passage in Libanius's speech *De patrociniis*, where he describes the support which they gave to certain large villages inhabited by free peasants, the excesses in which the villagers indulged, and the miserable situation of the city aristocracy, which was unable to collect any taxes from the peasants and was maltreated both by them and by the soldiers. Libanius, being himself a civilian and a large landowner, experienced all the discomfort of this *entente cordiale* between soldiery and peasants. The tenants on one of his own estates, perhaps in Judaea, who for four generations had not shown any sign of insubordination, became restless and tried, with the help of a higher officer, who was their patron, to dictate their own conditions of work to the landowner. Naturally Libanius is full of resentment and bitterness towards the soldiers and the officers. On the other hand, the support given by the troops to the villagers cannot be explained merely by greed. The soldiers in the provinces were still themselves peasants, and their officers were of the same origin. They were therefore in real sympathy with the peasants and were ready to help them against the despised inhabitants of the cities.

Some scattered evidence on the sharp antagonism between the peasants and the landowners of the cities may be found also in Egypt. In a typical document of the year A.D. 320 a magnate of the city of Hermupolis, a gymnasiarch and a member of the municipal council, Aurelius Adelphius, makes a complaint to the strategus of the nome. He was a hereditary lessee (ἐμφυτευτής) of γῆ οὐσιακή, a man who had inherited his estate from his father and had cultivated it all his life long. He had invested money in the land and improved its cultivation. When harvest-time arrived, the peasants of the village to the territory of which the estate belonged, "with the usual insolence of villagers" (κωμητικῇ αὐθαδίᾳ χρησάμενοι), tried to prevent him from gathering in the crop. The expression quoted shows how deep was the antagonism between city and country. It is not improbable that the "insolence" of the peasants is to be explained by their hopes of some support from outside. They may have been justified: the proprietor may have been a land-grabber who had deprived them of plots of land which they used to cultivate; but the point is the deep-rooted mutual hostility between the peasants and the landowners which the story reveals.

I feel no doubt, therefore, that the crisis of the third century was not political but definitely social in character. The city *bourgeoisie* had gradually replaced the aristocracy of Roman citizens, and the senatorial and the equestrian class was mostly recruited from its ranks. It was now attacked in turn by the masses of the peasants. In both cases the process was carried out by the army under the leadership of the emperors. The first act ended with the short but bloody revolution of A.D. 69–70, but it did not affect the foundations of the prosperity of the Empire, since the change was not a radical one. The second act, which had a much wider bearing, started the prolonged and calamitous crisis of the third century. Did this crisis end in a complete victory of the peasants over the city *bourgeoisie* and in the creation of a brand-new state? There is no question that the city *bourgeoisie,* as such, was crushed and lost the indirect influence on state affairs which it had exerted through the senate in the second century. Yet it did not disappear. The new ruling bureaucracy very soon established close social relations with the surviving remnant of this class, and the strongest and richest section of it still formed an important element of the imperial aristocracy. The class which was disappearing was the middle class, the active and thrifty citizens of the thousands of cities in the Empire, who formed the link between the lower and the upper classes. Of this class we hear very little after the catastrophe of the third century, save for the part which it played, as *curiales* of the cities, in the collection of taxes by the imperial government. It became more and more oppressed and steadily reduced in numbers.

While the *bourgeoisie* underwent the change we have described, can it be said that the situation of the peasants improved in consequence of their temporary victory? There is no shadow of doubt that in the end there were no victors in the terrible class war of this century. If the *bourgeoisie* suffered heavily, the peasants gained nothing. Anyone who reads the complaints of the peasants of Asia Minor and Thrace which have been quoted above, or the speeches of Libanius and the sermons of John Chrysostom and Salvian, or even the "constitutions" of the Codices of Theodosius and Justinian, will realize that in the fourth century the peasants were much worse off than they had been in the second. A movement which was started by envy and hatred, and carried on by murder and destruction, ended in such depression of spirit that any stable conditions seemed to the people preferable to unending anarchy. They therefore willingly accepted the stabilization brought about by Diocletian, regardless of the fact that it meant no improvement in the condition of the mass of the population of the Roman Empire.

F. W. Walbank

Trends in the Empire of the Second Century A.D.

I

The *pax Augusta* brought prosperity to a wide area of the earth's surface; but it completely failed to release new productive forces. As in the century after Alexander's death in 323 B.C. — a century in many ways comparable to the early Empire — the step to industrialization and the factory was never taken. Indeed, except for a few new devices like the mill-wheel, the level of technique inside the Roman Empire never surpassed that already reached at Alexandria. Nor was this due to any special Roman foible; on the contrary it continued the classical tradition of the Alexandrines, who could find no better use for many of their mechanical devices than to impress the ignorant congregations in the Egyptian temples and to bolster up their religion with sham miracles. For the origins of this tradition one must go back to the Greek city-state.

From its outset classical civilization inherited a low level of technical skill, judged by the part Greece and Rome were destined to play in history. The Greek tribes settled in a poor and rocky land; only by incessant labor could Hesiod wring a livelihood from the soil of Boeotia. Consequently, the leisure which was to bring forth the Ionian Renaissance and the fine flower of Periclean Athens could only be purchased at a price. The temples on the Acropolis, the plays in the theater of Dionysus, the speculations of Plato, were only possible because an army of women, resident foreigners, slaves and imperial subjects supported by their toil a leisured minority of full citizens. The position at Rome was similar. There the wealth of the late republic was built up . . . on the sweat of the provinces, the loot of many wars, and the sufferings of countless slaves enduring abject misery on the plantations of aristocratic landowners, resident in Rome. This relation-

Reprinted by permission of Lawrence and Wishart Ltd., from F. W. Walbank, *The Decline of the Roman Empire in the West* (New York, 1953), pp. 21–37, 67–69.

ship of absentee landlord and plantation slave reproduced in an accentuated form that contrast which underlay ancient civilization, between the leisured class of the city and the multitude laboring to support it on the land — a contrast which evoked a famous criticism of the cities of the Empire as "hives of drones."

This antithesis was no new thing; like the low level of classical technique, it had been characteristic of the ancient civilizations which sprang up in the river valleys of Egypt, Mesopotamia and the Punjab round about the third millennium B.C. Common to the east too was the institution of slavery, which spread from the home to the mine and the plantation, to become the basis of Greek and Roman civilization, a cancer in the flesh of society which grew with society itself. Slavery was never effectively challenged. Aristotle (384–322 B.C.), one of the most acute philosophers and students of political science who ever lived, laid it down as axiomatic that "from the hour of their birth some are marked out for subjection, others for rule" (*Politics*, I.5.2, 1254*a*); "the art of war" he wrote "is a natural art of acquisition, for it includes hunting, an art which we ought to practice against wild beasts and against men who, though intended by nature to be governed, will not submit; for war of such a kind is naturally just" (*Politics*, I.8.12, 1256*b*). It is perhaps not strange that a philosopher who so faithfully reflects the practice of his own society in framing his definition of a just war should also have sought to demonstrate the natural inferiority of woman to man.

After Aristotle another school of philosophers arose, the Stoics, who for a short time asserted the equality of slaves and free men; but they never passed from this to the obvious conclusion that slavery should be abolished. Very soon they too lapsed back into the easier Aristotelian view. Meanwhile slavery was spreading both geographically and in the number of human beings which it enveloped in its folds. The wars of Alexander's successors and of the Roman republic brought a constantly increasing supply; especially on the plantations and sheep ranches and in the mines they formed an indispensable source of labor. At Rome "Sardinians for sale" became a proverb for anything in cheap supply; and Strabo has left us a picture of the famous slave-market of Delos in the late second century B.C. (XIV, 668); "the island," he writes "could admit and send away tens of thousands of slaves in the same day. . . . The cause of this was the fact that the Romans, having become rich after the destruction of Carthage and Corinth (146 B.C.), used many slaves; and the pirates, seeing the easy profit therein, bloomed forth in great numbers, themselves not only going in quest of booty, but also trafficking in slaves."

It was this slavery at the root of society which controlled the general pattern of classical civilization. For it split up every community into two kinds of human beings — the free man and the slave; and it ordained that those who did the basic work of society should not be those to benefit from it. The natural outcome was that the slave lacked the incentive to master and improve the technique of the work he was doing. Equally disastrous was the effect upon the slaveowners themselves. Because it became normal to associate manual labor with slaves, Greek culture began to draw a line between the things of the hand and the things of the mind. In the *Republic*, Plato (*c.* 429–347 B.C.) pictured a utopian community divided into three sharply differentiated classes, endowed each with some imaginary "metallic" quality — Guardians with a golden cast of mind, to govern; Auxiliaries with an admixture of silver, to fight and police the state; and finally Workers, sharing in the base metals, to do the work of society and to obey. Aristotle, with an equal contempt for manual work, writes: "Doubtless in ancient times the artisan class were slaves or foreigners, and therefore the majority of them are so now. The best form of state will not admit them to citizenship" (*Politics*, III.5.3, 1278*a*). "Certainly the good man . . . and the good citizen ought not to learn the crafts of inferiors except for their own occasional use; if they habitually practice these, there will cease to be a distinction between master and slave" (*Politics*, III.4.13, 1277*b*).

The Roman attitude varied no whit from this. Cicero's formulation deserves to be quoted in full. "Public opinion," he writes (*De Officiis*, I, 150–51),

> *divides the trades and professions into the liberal and the vulgar. We condemn the odious occupation of the collector of customs and the usurer, and the base and menial work of unskilled laborers; for the very wages the laborer receives are a badge of slavery. Equally contemptible is the business of the retail dealer; for he cannot succeed unless he is dishonest, and dishonesty is the most shameful thing in the world. The work of the mechanic is also degrading; there is nothing noble about a workshop. The least respectable of all trades are those which minister to pleasure, as Terence tells us, "fishmongers, butchers, cooks, sausage-makers." Add to these if you like, perfumers, dancers, and the actors*

of the gaming-house. But the learned professions, such as medicine, architecture and the higher education, from which society derives the greatest benefit, are considered honorable occupations for those to whose social position they are appropriate. Business on a small scale is despicable; but if it is extensive and imports commodities in large quantities from all over the world and distributes them honestly, it is not so very discreditable; nay, if the merchant, satiated, or rather satisfied, with the fortune he has made, retires from the harbor and steps into an estate, as once he returned to harbor from the sea, he deserves, I think, the highest respect. But of all the sources of wealth farming is the best, the most able, the most profitable, the most noble.

Government at Rome throughout the period of the republic was in the hands of an aristocratic clique whose wealth was derived from land and which had debarred itself from commerce by a self-denying ordinance. This caste was the natural opponent of any economic improvement which challenged its own position. After the conquest of Macedonia in 168 B.C. it closed down the Macedonian mines lest they should strengthen the commercial elements which would have worked them; and once current needs could be met from the Spanish mines, the Senate practically stopped mining in Italy. "This maintained Senatorial authority beyond challenge: but it also checked the economic expansion which might have restored the balance in the country."

It was this landed class which peopled the countryside of Italy and Sicily with the slave gangs which later threatened Rome's very existence in the revolt of Spartacus (73–71 B.C.). Meanwhile the towns and cities were filling up with eastern slaves, who not only undertook all kinds of manual work, but also acted as teachers, doctors, architects and professional men. The consequence was that socially these activities were ill thought of. "The meaner sort of mechanic has a special and separate slavery," wrote Aristotle (*Politics*, I.13.13, 1260*a*); and similarly the Romans despised the free artisan as one doing work proper to a slave. Thus the atmosphere was wholly unfavorable to technical progress in a field for which anyone of any consequence had nothing but contempt. When labor is cheap and worthless, why conserve it? So the classical world perpetuated that technical retardation which had been one of the most paradoxical features of the civilizations of the Nile and Euphrates — paradoxical because it was thanks to a unique crop of technical inventions — the plow, the wheeled cart, the sailing boat, the solar calendar, the smelting of copper ores, the use of the power of oxen and the harnessing of the winds with sails — that these civilizations had come into being. In both instances the cause of retardation was the same — the bisection of society into classes with contrary interests.

Economically, this division of society ensured that the vast masses of the Empire never tasted the fruits of their labor; and this meant a permanently restricted internal market. Because wealth was concentrated at the top, the body of society suffered from chronic underconsumption. Accordingly industry had to seek its market either in the limited circle of the middle and upper class, together with the army (which therefore had considerable economic significance), or else outside the Empire, where of course there were even fewer markets for mass-produced goods. Consequently, the economic basis for industrialization was not to hand. The expansion of the Empire brought new markets, which staved off the problem for a time; but, as we shall see, the effects of this expansion were soon cancelled out by the decentralization of production and were never radical enough to carry a large-scale industry, using all the resources of advanced technique and advanced forms of power.

On the other hand, because of the social structure, Greece and Rome never even considered the possibility of catering for the proletariat and peasantry, and so creating a deeper, instead of a wider, market. What expansion the Empire brought proves on closer examination to be "a matter of greater extension, not of greater depth." The *pax Augusta* removed many handicaps and much wastage; goods circulated with greater ease and over wider areas. But there was no qualitative change in the nature of classical economy. In one field alone were there notable technical achievements — in that of building and engineering, where the Hellenistic Age had already given a lead, under the stimulus of interstate warfare; but even here the Romans were concerned with the amplifying and application of old processes rather than with the creation of new. Thus behind the rosy hues of Gibbon's picture of a prosperous Antonine world we are now in a position to detect at least one fatal weakness — the complete stagnation of technique.

II

It has been suggested above that in the long run the expansion of the Roman Empire could bring only a temporary fillip to its economy.

The reason why this was so deserves special attention, for it illuminates a factor of some importance for our central problem. Modern investigation has revealed in the Roman Empire the operation of an economic law which finds its application equally in our own society — the centrifugal tendency of industry to export itself instead of its products, and of trades to migrate from the older areas of the economy to the new.

The operation of this law has been felt with full force in this country, since India began to satisfy its own needs with cotton manufactured in Bombay; here the lesson has been underlined by mass unemployment in the cotton towns of Lancashire. Today this movement to the periphery is usually connected with the establishment of the capitalistic form of production in colonial and backward areas and, as such areas become independent states, these states use political methods to assert an economic independence based on local industry. "Autarky" as a feature of the national state is a characteristic of modern times. In the Roman Empire the factors were somewhat simpler and more primitive.

Perhaps the most important reason for moving industry as near as possible to the new market was the weakness of ancient communications. Judged by preceding ages, Roman communications were highly developed; but in relation to the tasks the Empire set, they were still far too primitive. Mechanically the vehicles used on land were very inefficient; for the ancient world never discovered the horsecollar, but employed a form of harness which half-strangled the beast every time it tried to drag a load along. A sea voyage was always chancy, and overseas trade a hazardous business. Even by the time of Augustus the task of maintaining imperial communications was beginning to weigh as an intolerable burden upon the inhabitants of the Empire. The cost of the Imperial Post, the upkeep of the roads, the housing of traveling officials — all these fell upon the provincial. And in spite of police and river flotillas, brigandage had not been wholly eliminated; the inns too were often poor and unevenly distributed. The difficulties of a voyage in the first century A.D. are illustrated by the story of St. Paul's adventures (including a shipwreck) on board the three vessels which were necessary to bring him from Palestine to Rome. In short, the best transport system of the ancient world was inadequate to cope with a relatively high circulation of consumer's goods; and to make matters worse there is evidence that deterioration had set in from the time of Augustus onwards.

A second factor which impelled industry outwards towards its markets was the insecurity of ancient credit. Because of the risks entailed, it was always costly to raise capital for a trading venture; interest rates were high because the risk run was personal. There was no ancient equivalent of the joint-stock company with limited liability to ensure corporate responsibility for financial ventures; and banking itself remained primitive. The Empire saw no further development of the Ptolemaic system of a central bank with branch establishments; on the contrary, in Egypt there are signs of regression to a system of independent local banks.

Furthermore, the fact that ancient industry was based on slavery also influenced the movement of decentralization. For slavery as an institution was adversely affected by the Augustan peace. The steps the emperors took to end war and piracy caused a drying-up of the main source of supply. The great days of the Delian slave market were gone forever; and, though under the more humane conditions of the early Empire the number of home-reared slaves was quite considerable, they were not sufficient to fill the gap, so that increasingly the Roman world had to fall back on the small trickle from outside the frontiers. Besides this, the growth of humanitarian sentiment . . . led to a widespread movement of slave-manumission. Yesterday's slave was tomorrow's freedman; and his grandsons would be full Roman citizens. Clearly the normal basis of ancient capitalistic activity was being undermined. And this led to a shifting of industry to more primitive lands where, as in Gaul, industry had available, if not new slaves, what was perhaps better, a free proletariat willing to turn its hands to manual labor. In the Celtic lands, as in Ptolemaic Egypt, we find free workers engaged in industrial production. Whereas in the potteries of Arretium in Italy, before A.D. 25, 123 out of 132 known workers were slaves, there is no evidence for the employment of slaves in the potteries of Gaul and the Rhine valley; and inscriptions from Dijon refer to stoneworkers and smiths as "free dependents" *(clientes)* of a local *seigneur* — an interesting sidelight on the breakup of the tribal system and the growth of social classes in Gaul. This shifting of industry contributed to the already mentioned urbanization of these backward parts; and here we may note that the new municipalities in such areas as Gaul and Spain inherited what the Italian municipalities had largely lost — a hinterland inhabited by peasants. It has been argued that by becoming each a little Rome in exploiting the dwellers in its own countryside the municipalities contributed on a long-term view to their own subsequent ruin.

Another important feature of industry based on slavery was that concentration brought no appreciable reduction of overhead expenses, as happens where power-machines are employed. Hence there was no incentive to develop the old centers rather than expand to new. Moreover, the simple nature of ancient equipment, the absence of complicated machinery, made it a comparatively easy business to move. Usually it would merely be a question of a few simple tools and the skill carried in a man's own fingers. On the other hand, the restricted internal market, which necessarily drove the merchant farther and farther afield, combined with the constant demands of a relatively prosperous army along the frontiers to reinforce the general centrifugal tendency of industry. Incidentally, the army had changed its economic role since the days of the republic. Then, as the source of valuable plunder, it had paid its way over and over again; now, as a peaceful garrison force, rarely fighting, and then against poor barbarians, it was an economic liability, some 250,000 to 300,000 — rising later to 400,000 and more — idle mouths to feed — an item which must certainly figure among the causes of Roman decline.

All these tendencies did not operate at once nor to the same extent; but over a period of years they resulted in a clear movement of industry outwards from the old centers of the Empire. One of the earliest developments was that trade became local and provincial instead of international; though, significantly, the drop in long-distance trade in mass-produced goods did not apply to luxury articles, which still traveled virtually any distance to meet the demands of the wealthy few. Over the whole Empire there was a gradual reversion to small-scale, hand-to-mouth craftsmanship, producing for the local market and for specific orders in the vicinity. Often the movement of decentralization had two stages. Thus the manufacture of *terra sigillata*, the universal red-ware pottery of the early Empire, shifted first from Italy to Graufesenque in the Cevennes and thence, in the course of the second century A.D., to Lezoux in the Allier basin, to eastern Gaul, Rhaetia and Alsace, and finally to Rheinzabern near Speyer. "In the African lamp industry Italian wares gave place to Carthaginian, which themselves lost the market to lamps of purely local manufacture."

The progress made by the various provinces was naturally uneven;

sometimes the first result of decentralization was to locate some important manufacture in particularly favorable surroundings; in which case the decentralized industry might for a time capture the international market. This happened to Gallic wine and pottery, which were exported from Narbonne and Arles to the east, until the middle of the third century; pottery from Gaul is found throughout this period in Italy, Spain, Africa, Britain and even in Syria and Egypt. But on the whole this was exceptional, and in the case of Gaul and Germany was probably due to geographical factors, especially the excellent water-transport system, and also to the existence of cheap labor, conditions which were not reproduced in the older provinces of the east.

Progress in such areas as Gaul and Roman Germany was balanced by the decay of Italy. During the second century A.D. this one-time kernel of the Empire lost increasingly its predominant position. Northern Italy remained prosperous for a longer period, thanks to its links with the Danube provinces. But in the rest of the peninsula from the end of the first century A.D. onwards there appear signs of depopulation and a marked decline in the export of both agricultural and industrial products. As the trend towards decentralization developed, and as the Gallic wine-trade grew, the vineyards and olive fields of Italy shrank, making place increasingly for the cultivation of corn on large estates, farmed with serf-labor. Italy became an incubus, supported by invisible exports — officials' salaries and the Emperor's private income.

Simultaneously, at the opposite extreme, in the lands outside the frontiers, and especially to the north and northeast, among the Gauls, the Germans and the Scythians, the outward expansion of Roman trade and influence was inducing a ferment, which was to have the most far-reaching effects. Already the Gauls whom Caesar conquered (59–50 B.C.) and the Germans whom Tacitus described in his *Germania*, published in A.D. 98, had to some degree modified their earlier tribal organization; in both lands there were considerable differences of wealth, and rich counts had each their retinues of followers. But from the time of Augustus the natural development of these peoples was accelerated by the impact of Romanization. Increasingly they became involved in imperial trade currents, buying and selling across the frontiers. Increasingly they enlisted in the Roman armies as mercenaries, and on retirement took their Roman habits back to their tribes like New Guinea natives returning home from Rabaul or Sydney. Romanized chieftains employed their new culture in the service of Rome, or like

Arminius, against her. In short, the centrifugal economic movement did not and could not stop at the frontiers; but overflowing into the barbarian world beyond, it carried the virtues and vices of civilization like a strong wine to unaccustomed heads. Thus it was the Romans themselves who taught the northern barbarians to look with interest and envy at the rich spoils of the Empire.

Meanwhile the process of decentralization and subdivision into smaller and smaller local economic units could have only one ultimate result — provincial autarky and the decomposition of the Empire. As one might expect, this economic tendency found its political reflection in the division of the Empire, first of all in the fourfold administration of Diocletian and his three colleagues (A.D. 286), later, after Constantine had transferred the capital to Byzantium (A.D. 330), in the permanent division into an eastern and western Empire, which laid the foundations of medieval Europe.

III

Fundamental too for medieval Europe was one particular aspect of this general movement of decentralization — the gradual transfer of industry from the cities to the villages and large country estates. In this way the essentially agrarian character of ancient civilization began to reassert itself over the urban elements which had produced its highest and most typical developments; the depressed countryside took its revenge for the long centuries during which its needs were subordinated to those of the smart men of the towns. In Italy, as we saw, vineyards and olive gardens now began to make way for large corn-growing estates; in short, intensive cultivation gave way to a less efficient and less specialized system.

Since the early days of the republic the large estate had never at any time been exceptional in the Roman world: during the Civil War of 49 B.C., Caesar records (*Bell. Civ.* I, 17) how Domitius Ahenobarbus, one of Pompey's generals, attempted to ensure his soldiers' allegiance in a tight corner by promising 1,500 men between two and three acres each out of his own private estates; and in Nero's reign, Pliny tells us (*Nat. Hist.* XVIII, 35), six men owned half the province of Africa. But then there had been countertendencies such as the granting of small allotments to retired veterans, which worked in the direction of peasant holdings. Before long these allotments ceased; and increasingly the large estate became the typical unit. Moreover it began to develop in a way which ultimately transformed its character altogether, and with it the whole system of classical economy.

In the first place, the large country estate had always been the scene of a certain amount of industry. Specially trained slaves had done the necessary farm jobs, tanning, weaving, wagon-making, fulling and work in the carpenter's or blacksmith's shop. By A.D. 50 Pliny assumes the presence of such craftsmen to be a normal feature of any estate; and by the time of Vespasian (A.D. 69–79) the emperor's own estates, organized on the pattern of the royal domains of the Hellenistic period, were setting the fashion in the provinces by becoming increasingly an agglomeration of craftsmen of every kind, as well as agricultural laborers — in fine, a self-contained community of a type common to the old Bronze Age civilizations, and later, as the manor, to medieval Christendom. Here too the regression was by no means along a straight line. Indeed, as the self-contained estate becomes increasingly a feature of the countryside of Africa, S. Russia, Italy, Asia Minor, Babylonia, Palestine and Syria, it is remarkable to watch it not simply asserting its self-sufficiency, but actually going into competition with the towns to capture the international market. With the general crisis of the third century, which hit the towns hardest, it was on such estates that economic life remained most vigorous.

The gradual drying-up of the sources of slave labor compelled the landowner to seek some other supply. Increasingly he turned to the *coloni*, not sturdy independent peasants of the old Italian type, but tenant farmers, successors of the obsolescent slave class to the doubtful privilege of being the bottom dog in the countryside. These *coloni* were usually too poor to pay rent for their land or to buy their own implements and seed; these they obtained from the landlord and, as "sharecroppers," repaid him in kind and, in some provinces such as Africa, by services on his private land. Subsistence agriculture along these lines required neither traditional skill nor experience: it offered the "new rich," who arose out of the various crises of the state, an opportunity to increase their fortunes in a safe and easy fashion.

The factor of inadequate transport, already considered above, also helped the growth of these self-sufficient, "oriental," industrial estates. By making everything on the spot, the late Roman precursor of the feudal baron would eliminate the most costly item in his bill of expenses. It is not surprising that this sort of "nuclear" economy tended to attach itself to any kind of large unit engaged in primary production.

It was as if industry had lost all confidence in its ability to stand alone, and must seek the prop and protection of forms of livelihood nearer to the basic needs of mankind. Not only large agricultural estates, but also mining camps, fisheries and hunting parks became to an increasing extent the nuclei around which handicrafts and industries agglomerated themselves. Sometimes these primary units were temple property, not only recalling the similar institutions of Babylon or Hellenistic Asia Minor, but also foreshadowing clearly the medieval monastery. Similarly, the new, depressed class of *coloni* were the forerunners of the later serfs.

From the time of Augustus onwards this form of "domain" economy was encroaching gradually upon the old capitalist system, based on slave labor and the free market; and it was soon followed by a catastrophic drop in every branch of agricultural technique. It is significant that after the first century A.D. agricultural literature ceased to exist as a creative force, and in its place we find the mechanical transcribing of ancient works. Yet, notwithstanding this decline in the efficiency of agricultural technique, the land continued to exercise a magnetic attraction as conditions in the towns deteriorated. . . . The State found itself obliged to make ever greater financial demands upon the bourgeoisie. From this pressure, the "nuclear" estate, worked by the methods of subsistence economy, offered its owner a safe retreat. In the late third century A.D. the Talmud directs its readers to keep a third of their estate in land, a third in cash at home, and a third invested in commerce and industry — advice which implies a recognition of the breakdown of capitalistic production and even of money economy.

This flight of industry from the towns to the manorial estates itself contributed to the general economic breakdown by reducing the effective areas open to trade. Each estate, in proportion as it became self-sufficing, meant so many more individuals subtracted from the classical economic system, so many less potential consumers for those commodities which still circulated on the old markets. So the large domain played its part in restricting trade and speeding up the general process of decentralization.

By now it must be apparent that Gibbon's picture of Rome under the Antonines needs considerable qualification. For we have traced several factors of decline rooted in the structure of Roman society, which were already beginning to operate from the time of Augustus (27 B.C. — A.D. 14), and were certainly in full swing during the period which Gibbon praised for its unique felicity. We have seen how the low level of technique in Graeco-Roman civilization had led to the development of slavery as a means of purchasing the leisure necessary for comfort and culture; and how this institution operated on both slave and master to rule out the possibility of releasing new productive forces on a scale adequate to change the material conditions of society. We have seen the restricted internal market, which followed inevitably from a social structure of this kind, bringing its own nemesis in the shape of an outward drive to seek fresh markets away from the old centers of civilization. We have seen how the backwardness of credit institutions and of communications, and the drying-up of the slave supply itself, served to reinforce this decentralizing movement, which was eventually to end in the political disintegration of the Empire. And finally we have noted the growth of the large estate, the symbol of the decline of urban civilization, and both a result of the general decay and a factor hastening it.

The cause of the decline of the Roman Empire is not to be sought in any one feature — in the climate, the soil, the health of the population, or indeed in any of those social and political factors which played so important a part in the actual process of decay — but rather in the whole structure of ancient society. The date at which the contradictions, which were ultimately to prove fatal, first began to appear is not A.D. 200 nor yet the setting-up of the Principate by Augustus Caesar in 27 B.C., but rather the fifth century B.C. when Athens revealed her inability to keep and broaden the middle-class democracy she had created. The failure of Athens epitomized the failure of the city-state. Built on a foundation of slave labor, or on the exploitation of similar groups, including the peasantry, the city-state yielded a brilliant minority civilization. But from the start it was topheavy. Through no fault of its citizens, but as a result of the time and place when it arose, it was supported by a woefully low level of technique. To say this is to repeat a truism. The paradoxical contrast between the spiritual achievements of Athens and her scanty material goods has long been held up to the admiration of generations who had found that a rich material inheritance did not automatically ensure richness of cultural life. But it was precisely this low level of technique, relative to the tasks Greek and Roman society set itself, that made it impossible even to consider dispensing with slavery and led to its extension from the harmless sphere of domestic labor to the mines and workshops, where it grew stronger as the contradictions of society became more apparent.

As so often, we find ourselves discussing as cause and effect factors which were constantly interacting, so that in reality the distinction between the effective agent and the result it brought about is often quite arbitrary. But roughly speaking, the city-state, precisely because it was a minority culture, tended to be aggressive and predatory, its claim to autonomy sliding over insensibly, at every opportunity, into a claim to dominate others. This led to wars, which in turn took their place among the many sources of fresh slaves. Slavery grew, and as it invaded the various branches of production it led inevitably to the damping down of scientific interest, to the cleavage, already mentioned, between the classes that used their hands and the superior class that used — and later ceased using — its mind. This ideological cleavage thus reflects a genuine separation of the community into classes; and henceforward it becomes the supreme task of even the wisest sons of the city-state — a Plato and an Aristotle — to maintain this class society, whatsoever the cost.

That cost was indeed heavy. It says much for Plato's singlemindedness that he was willing to meet it. In the *Laws*, his last attempt to plan the just city, he produces a blueprint for implanting beliefs and attitudes convenient to authority through the medium of suggestion, by a strict and ruthless censorship, the substitution of myths and emotional ceremonies for factual knowledge, the isolation of the citizen from the outside world, the creation of types with standardized reactions, and, as a final guarantee, by the sanctions of the police-state, to be invoked against all who cannot or will not conform.

Such was the intellectual and spiritual fruit of this tree, whose roots had split upon the hard rock of technical inadequacy. Materially, the result of increasing slavery was the certainty that new productive forces would not be released on any scale sufficient for a radical transformation of society. Extremes of wealth and poverty became more marked, the internal market flagged, and ancient society suffered a decline of trade and population and, finally, the wastage of class warfare. Into this sequence the rise of the Roman Empire brought the new factor of a parasitical capital; and it spread the Hellenistic system to

Italy, where agrarian pauperism went side by side with imperial expansion and domination on an unparalleled scale.

From all this arose the typical developments of the social life of the Empire — industrial dispersion and a reversion to agrarian self-sufficiency — and the final attempt to retrieve the crisis, or at least to salvage whatever could be salvaged from the ruins, by the unflinching use of oppression and the machinery of the bureaucratic state. These tendencies we have already analyzed, and need not repeat them here. The important point is that they fall together into a sequence with its own logic, and that they follow — not of course in the specific details, which were determined by a thousand personal or fortuitous factors, but in their general outlines — from the premises upon which classical civilization arose, namely an absolutely low technique and, to compensate for this, the institution of slavery. Herein lie the real causes of the decline and fall of the Roman Empire.

Salvian the Presbyter

The Burden of Taxation

Salvian the Presbyter lived in the province of Gaul in the fifth century and experienced the consequences of the German invasions. His book *On the Governance of God*, written in 440, contrasted the uncorrupted excellence of the barbarians with the decadence of the Roman Empire. In the following selection he tells of the heavy burden of taxation born by the people of the empire.

But what else can these wretched people wish for, they who suffer the incessant and even continuous destruction of public tax levies. To them there is always imminent a heavy and relentless proscription. They

From *The Writings of Salvian, The Presbyter*, trans. Jeremiah F. O'Sullivan, from *Fathers of the Church*, Vol. 3, Catholic University of America Press, 1947. Reprinted by permission of the publisher.

desert their homes, lest they be tortured in their very homes. They seek exile, lest they suffer torture. The enemy is more lenient to them than the tax collectors. This is proved by this very fact, that they flee to the enemy in order to avoid the full force of the heavy tax levy. This very tax levying, although hard and inhuman, would nevertheless be less heavy and harsh if all would bear it equally and in common. Taxation is made more shameful and burdensome because all do not bear the burden of all. They exort tribute from the poor man for the taxes of the rich, and the weaker carry the load for the stronger. There is no other reason that they cannot bear all the taxation except that the burden imposed on the wretched is greater than their resources.

They suffer from envy and want, which are misfortunes most diverse and unlike. Envy is bound up with payment of the tax; need, with the ability to pay. If you look at what they pay, you will think them abundant in riches, but if you look at what they actually possess, you will find them poverty stricken. Who can judge an affair of this wretchedness? They bear the payment of the rich and endure the poverty of beggars. Much more serious is the following: the rich themselves occasionally make tributary levies which the poor pay.

But, you say, when the assessment due from the rich is very heavy and the taxes due from them are very heavy, how does it happen that they wish to increase their own debt? I do not say that they increase the taxes for themselves. They increase them because they do not increase them for themselves. I will tell you how this is done. Commonly, new envoys, new bearers of letters, come from the imperial offices and those men are recommended to a few well-known men for the mischief of many. For them new gifts are decreed, new taxes are decreed. The powerful levy what the poor are to pay, the courtesy of the rich decrees what the multitude of the wretched are to lose. They themselves in no way feel what they levy.

You say they who were sent by our superiors cannot be honored and generously entertained otherwise. Therefore, you rich men, you who are the first to levy, be the first to give. Be the first in generosity of goods, you who are the first in profusion of words. You who give of mine, give of thine. Most justly, whoever you are, you who alone wish to receive favor, you alone should bear the expense. But to your will, O rich men, we the poor accede. What you, the few, order, we all pay. What is so just, so humane? Your decrees burden us with new debts; at least make your debt common to us all. What is more wicked and more unworthy than that you alone are free from debt, you who make us all debtors?

Indeed, the most wretched poor thus pay all that I have mentioned, but for what cause or for what reason they pay, they are completely ignorant. For, to whom is it lawful to discuss why they pay; to whom is permitted to find out what is owed? Then it is given out most publicly when the rich get angry with each other, when some of them get indignant because some levies are made without their advice and handling.

Then you may hear it said by some of them, "What an unworthy crime! Two or three decree what kills many; what is paid by many wretched men is decreed by a few powerful men." Each rich man maintains his honor by being unwilling that anything is decreed in his absence, yet he does not maintain justice by being unwilling that evil things be done when he is present. Lastly, what these very men consider base in others they themselves later legalize, either in punishment of a past contempt or in proof of their power. Therefore, the most unfortunate poor are, as it were, in the midst of the sea, between conflicting, violent winds. They are swamped by the waves rolling now from one side, now from the other.

But, surely, those who are wicked in one way are found moderate and just in another, and compensate for their baseness in one thing by goodness in another. For, just as they weigh down the poor with the burden of new tax levies, so they sustain them by the assistance of new tax reliefs; just as the lower classes are oppressed by new taxes, so they are equally relieved by tax mitigations. Indeed, the injustice is equal in taxes and reliefs, for, as the poor are the first to be burdened, so they are the last to be relieved.

For when, as has happened lately, the highest powers thought it would be advisable that taxation should be lessened somewhat for the cities which were in arrears in their payments, the rich alone instantly divided among themselves the remedy given for all. Who, then, remembers the poor? Who calls the poor and needy to share in the common benefit? Who permits him who is first in bearing the burden even to stand in the last place for receiving redress? What more is there to say? In no way are the poor regarded as taxpayers, unless when the mass of taxes is imposed upon them; they are not reckoned among the number of taxpayers when the tax-reliefs are portioned.

Do we think we are unworthy of the punishment of divine severity when we thus constantly punish the poor? Do we think, when we are constantly wicked, that God should not exercise His justice against all of us? Where or in whom are evils so great, except among the Romans? Whose injustice so great except our own? The Franks are ignorant of this crime of injustice. The Huns are immune to these crimes. There are no wrongs among the Vandals and none among the Goths. So far are the barbarians from tolerating these injustices among the Goths, that not even the Romans who live among them suffer them.

Therefore, in the districts taken over by the barbarians, there is one desire among all the Romans, that they should never again find it necessary to pass under Roman jurisdiction. In those regions, it is the one and general prayer of the Roman people that they be allowed to carry on the life they lead with the barbarians. And we wonder why the Goths are not conquered by our portion of the population, when the Romans prefer to live among them rather than with us. Our brothers, therefore, are not only altogether unwilling to flee to us from them, but they even cast us aside in order to flee to them.

G. E. M. de Ste. Croix

The "Decline and Fall": An Explanation

Geoffrey Ernest Maurice de Ste. Croix was born in 1910. He was educated at University College, London, and Oxford University. He served in the RAF during the Second World War and taught in England and the Netherlands before taking up an appointment as Fellow and Tutor in Ancient History at New College, Oxford, in 1953, posts that he held until his retirement in 1977. His most important works are *The Origins of the Peloponnesian War* (1972) and *The Class Struggle in the Ancient Greek World* (1981).

What a terrifying individual he could be is nicely illustrated in one of those Lives of Saints from which so much of our information about the lives and outlook of the poor in the Later Roman Empire is derived: the *Life of St. John the Almsgiver*, . . . If we want to characterise a cruel and merciless person, we sometimes say, "He's like a wild beast." Well, the Saint is represented as thinking about the dreadful monsters he may meet after death, and the only way he can adequately express the appalling ferocity of these wild beasts is to say that they will be "like tax-collectors." Certainly, tax collection from the poor in Roman times was not a matter of polite letters and, as a last resort, a legal action: beating-up defaulters was a matter of routine, if they were humble people. A casual remark of the fifth-century ecclesiastical writer Theodoret shows us what the procedure of tax-collection was likely to be in a Syrian village: "At this time," he says, "collectors (*praktores*) arrived, who compelled them to pay their taxes and began to imprison some and maltreat others." . . . In Egypt the same brutal procedure can be seen at work: local officials would seize taxpayers whom they alleged (rightly or wrongly) to be in default, imprison and ill-treat them, and, with the aid of soldiers and local levies, burn down their houses. After quoting a particular example of such a procedure, from the reign of Justinian, Sir Harold Bell (a leading papyrologist and historian of Graeco-Roman Egypt) remarked, "Such, to judge by other evidence, were regular accompaniments to the process of collecting arrears of taxes from an Egyptian village in the sixth century." According to Ammianus, an Egyptian in the late fourth century would blush for shame if he could not show on his back scars inflicted by the tax-collector's whip. . . . And it is worth repeating here the statement of Ammianus . . . that the Emperor Julian realised it was no good granting remissions of tax arrears in Gaul in the 350s, because this would only benefit the rich; the poor would have been made to pay immediately and in full. . . . There must have been many occasions, too, on which hapless peasants were forced to pay their taxes twice over, whether because the tax had first been extracted from them by the agents of a "usurper," . . . or because their landlord, after collecting the tax, became insolvent before paying it over to the authorities (or the persons to whom he was responsible). There is an example of the latter situation in a letter of Pope Gregory the Great, written in 591, from which we learn that the *rustici* on an estate of the Roman Church in Sicily had been compelled to pay their *burdatio* twice to the head lessee,

Theodosius, now almost insolvent. Gregory, an exceptionally conscientious landlord, orders that the 57 solidi concerned are to be repaid to the peasants as a prior claim against Theodosius' estate. . . .

It will be objected that the appalling situation I have been describing is characteristic only of the Later Empire, and that things were surely very different under the Principate, especially in the first two centuries of the Christian era. Certainly, taxation became much heavier in the fourth century onwards. . . . But there is no reason to think that defaulting taxpayers who were poor men, especially peasants, would be much better treated in the first century than in the fourth, although, until certain of the privileges of the Roman citizenship became in practice limited to the upper classes, during the second century, . . . the Roman citizen who was a person of no consequence might occasionally be able to assert his legal rights. (St. Paul did so, as we have seen — but of course he was far from being an uneducated peasant.) The native villager, especially if he was not a Roman citizen (as very few villagers were in the Greek-speaking part of the empire before 212), would have had little chance of escaping any brutal treatment which soldiers or officials cared to inflict upon him. There is a certain amount of evidence pointing in this direction, of which I will single out one text, quoted by several modern writers. Philo of Alexandria writes of events which he represents as having taken place "recently" (and therefore presumably during the reign of Tiberius, 14–37), apparently in Lower Egypt, as a result of the activity of a rapacious and cruel tax-collector:

> *When some who appeared to be defaulting merely through sheer poverty took to flight, in dread of severe punishment, he forcibly carried off their women and children and parents and other relatives, beat them, and subjected them to every kind of outrage. Although they were unable either to reveal the fugitive's whereabouts or (because of their own destitution) to pay what was due from him, he persisted, torturing them and putting them to death in a cruel manner. Others committed suicide to avoid such a fate. When there were no relatives left, he extended his outrages to neighbours and sometimes even to villages and towns, which were rapidly deserted by the flight of their inhabitants to places where they hoped to escape detection. . . .*

Even if we make the necessary allowance for Philo's characteristic exaggeration, a grim picture emerges; and, as Bell has said, "records found in Egypt have brought us proof that there is substantial truth in

Philo's statements" . . . . We must admit, with Philo, that such outrages, not only against the property but against the bodies and even the lives of those unfortunates who are seized in substitution for the actual debtors are only too likely when the annual collection of taxes is in the hands of "men of barbarous nature, who have never tasted of human culture and are obeying tyrannical orders." . . .

Some of the numerous complaints about taxation in the literary sources for the Later Roman Empire are of course over-coloured; their exaggerations are often traceable to political or religious spite, or to a desire to flatter the current emperor by damning his predecessors. However, anyone who is inclined to discount the admittedly very rhetorical evidence of the literary sources should read some of the imperial legislation. A particularly interesting specimen is the *Second Novel* (issued on 11 March 458) of the last great Western emperor, the young Majorian, of whom Stein said that we could "admire in him without reserve the last figure possessing a real grandeur in the history of the Roman West." . . . Although this Novel was issued only in the West, the situation it depicts, *mutatis mutandis*, prevailed also in the Greek East, where the oppression of the vast majority was effected in ways that were basically similar, even if it did not reach quite the same degree of intensity. The Novel is well worth reading as a whole; but it is long, and I can do no more than summarise parts of it. . . . The Novel is entitled "On the remission of arrears [of tax]," *De indulgentiis reliquorum*. It begins by stressing the woes of the provincials, whose fortunes are said to have been enfeebled and worn down, not only by the exaction of the various forms of regular tribute but also by extraordinary fiscal burdens (*extraordinaria onera*, *superindictitii tituli*), and the necessity of purchasing deferments — by bribing officials. A nice abstract phrase, *sub impossibili devotione*, characterises the plight of the landowner (*possessor*), drained of resources (*exhaustus*) and unable to discharge his arrears of tax, when confronted with yet another demand that "dutiful as he is, he cannot fulfil." With the exception of one minor tax in kind, a general remission of arrears is granted, explicitly for the benefit of the landowners (*possessores*), who are conceived as responsible for all taxes. Even if payment has been undertaken by someone else (no doubt at a high rate of interest), perhaps on the faith of a solemn promise by *stipulatio* by the taxpayer, the latter is still to have relief. . . . The Novel goes on to boast that the emperor has "put an end to the harshness of the ferocious tax collectors." There is a bitter complaint that the staffs of the highest officials of the state (those of the praetorian prefects are singled out) range around the provinces, and "by enormous exactions terrorise the landowner and the decurion," accounting for only a small proportion of the taxes they collect and, greedy and swollen with power as they are, extorting twice as much or more by way of commission (*sportulae*) for themselves. . . . In the good old days, Majorian adds, tax collection had been carried out, through the local councils, by the office staff of the provincial governor, who were fairly humble men and whom the governor could keep in order. But now the collection was in the hands of emissaries of the central "palatine" administration, described by the emperor as "terrible with the prestige of their exalted official rank, raging against the vitals of the provincials, to their ruin," and able to snap their fingers at a mere provincial governor. (Majorian was not by any means the first emperor, or the last, to complain about the intervention of central government officials in provincial taxation procedures.) Because of the oppression of these high officials, the emperor goes on, the cities have been despoiled of their councillors and can provide no qualified decurion; and the landowners, terrified by the atrocious behaviour of the financial officials, are deserting their country estates, as they are faced not merely with the loss of their fortunes but with "severe imprisonment and cruel tortures" inflicted upon them by the merciless officials for their own profit, with military aid. The collection of taxes must be entrusted once more to the provincial governors, and there must be no more interventions by palatine officials and the military, except to encourage governors to do their duty. The emperor stresses again . . . that he is making this ordinance as a remedy for the landowner (*pro remedio possessoris*). He proceeds to complain also . . . of "the men of power" (*potentes personae*), whose agents throughout the provinces neglect to pay their taxes, and who remain contumaciously on their estates, secure against any summons in the fear inspired by their arrogance. The agents and overseers of those families which are "senatorial or powerful" must submit themselves to the jurisdiction of the provincial governors (as they had not been doing), and so must the local agents in charge of estates belonging to the imperial household. Moreover, . . . provincial governors must not be subjected to molestation by false accusations from the staffs of the great officers of state, who will be furious at having enormously profitable spoils wrested from their own fraudulent grasp.

Some other laws of the fifth and sixth centuries unloose similar streams of righteous indignation at much the same objectives: see, for example, Valentinian III's *Novel* . . . (of 450), followed . . . by an ingenuous remark which reveals the main reason for the emperor's solicitude for the *possessores*: "A landowner who has been made poor is lost to us; one who is not overburdened is useful to us"! There are several similarly revealing laws, notably, for the East, the long *Eighth Novel* of Justinian, of A.D. 535, . . . Justinian too is concerned lest excessive exploitation by the great men, and their imposition of extraordinary burdens, should impair the ability of his subjects to pay their regular taxation, which he calls not only "accustomed and legal" but also "pious" (*eusebeis phoroi*, . . .). Similarly, the anxiety shown by Justinian in a series of three *Novels* in 535 to protect the free peasants of the praetorian prefecture of Illyricum and the provinces of Thracian Haemimontus and Moesia Secunda against money-lenders . . . is very likely to have been due in large part to anxiety to preserve them as an important source of recruitment for the army, as we know they were in his reign.

The laws I have been describing nicely illustrate the most fundamental reason why it was necessary to have an emperor in the first place. . . . The Principate was accepted (if at first with some grumbling) by the Roman (and Greek) propertied classes because on the whole they realised that their own privileged position might be imperilled if too many individuals among their number were allowed, as in the Late Republic, to plunder the empire too freely. If that happened, civil wars (accompanied, as they could well be, by proscriptions and confiscations) and even perhaps revolutions from below might destroy many of them. The situation could hardly be put better than in Machiavelli's statement, which I have quoted, about the necessity for having, "where the material is so corrupt, . . . besides laws, a superior force, such as appertains to a monarch, who has such absolute and overwhelming power that he can restrain excesses due to ambition and the corrupt practices of the powerful." . . . In the Later Empire, the *potentés*, *potentiores* or *dynatoi*, the men of power, became harder to control and often defied or circumvented the emperors with impunity. Senators, at once the richest and the most influential group in the empire, were more easily able than anyone to delay or avoid payment of their taxes and the fulfilment of their other liabilities. This was true even in the Eastern part of the empire. In 397, for example, an edict of the Emperor Arcadius, addressed to the praetorian prefect of the East, complained that in some provinces half of the taxes due from senators were in arrear. . . . In the West, where the senators were even richer and more powerful, this situation was worse. In the very same year, 397, when the revolt of Gildo in Africa had imperilled the corn supply of Rome itself, three very significant laws were issued in the West, where the young Emperor Honorius was dominated by his able *magister militum* Stilicho. The first, in June, ordered that not even imperial estates should be exempted from the obligation to supply recruits in person. . . . The second and third, in September and November, weakly conceded, in response to senatorial objections, that senators alone (even if head lessees of imperial estates) should have the right to commute their liability to supply recruits and pay in gold instead. . . . And as late as the early sixth century we find an edict drafted by Cassiodorus for Theodoric the Ostrogoth, then king of Italy, deploring the fact that Roman senators, who "ought to be setting an example," had paid virtually none of the taxes due from them, thus leaving the poor (the *tenues*) to bear an intolerable burden. . . .

The texts I have been quoting illustrate very well how the "government" was continually frustrated in such attempts as it did make (for whatever reasons) to protect the peasantry by the fact that the more important of the officials on whom it was obliged to rely to carry out its orders were themselves members of the upper class, and of course felt an instinctive sympathy with its other members and often connived at their malpractices, and indeed were guilty of much extortion themselves. The rulers of the empire rarely if ever had any real concern for the poor and unprivileged as such; but they sometimes realised the necessity to give some of them some protection (as we have just seen), either to prevent them from being utterly ruined and thus become useless as taxpayers, or to preserve them as potential recruits for the army. Try as they would, however, the emperors had no choice but to act through the officials I have just characterised as members of the exploiting class. No text that I know speaks more eloquently of the defects of this system than a Novel of the Emperor Romanus II issued between 959 and 963: "We must beware lest we send upon the unfortunate poor the calamity of law-officers, more merciless than famine itself."

Over all, no one I think will doubt that the position of humble folk in the Graeco-Roman world became distinctly worse after the early Principate. I have described . . . how their *Rechtsstellung* deteriorated during the first two centuries; and . . . I have shown how even the lower ranges of the curial order (falling only just inside, and sometimes perhaps even a little below, my "propertied class") were subjected to increasing fiscal oppression from the second half of the second century onwards, and during the latter part of the fourth century lost at least one of their most valuable privileges: exemption from flogging. It need not surprise us when we are told that in the numerous papyri of the Later Roman Empire from the Oxyrhynchus area the use of the Greek word *doulos*, once the standard technical term for "slave," is almost confined to occasions on which humble members of the free population are referring to themselves when addressing people of higher standing. . . .

I hope it is now clear how I would explain, through a class analysis, the ultimate disintegration of a large part of the Roman empire — although of course a Greek core, centered above all in Asia Minor, did survive for centuries. I would keep firmly in view the process of exploitation which is what I mean primarily when I speak of a "class struggle." As I see it, the Roman political system (especially when Greek democracy had been wiped out, . . .) facilitated a most intense and ultimately destructive economic exploitation of the great mass of the people, whether slave or free, and it made radical reform impossible. The result was that the propertied class, the men of real wealth, who had deliberately created this system for their own benefit, drained the life-blood from their world and thus destroyed Graeco-Roman civilisation over a large part of the empire — Britain, Gaul, Spain and north Africa in the fifth century; much of Italy and the Balkans in the sixth; and in the seventh, Egypt, Syria and Mesopotamia, and again north Africa, which had been reconquered by Justinian's generals in the sixth century. That, I believe, was the principal reason for the decline of Classical civilisation. I would suggest that the causes of the decline were above all economic and social. The very hierarchical political structure of the Roman empire, of course, played an important part; but it was precisely the propertied class as such which in the long run monopolised political power, with the definite purpose of maintaining and increasing its share of the comparatively small surplus which could be extracted from the primary producers. By non-Marxist historians this process has normally been described as if it were a more or less automatic one, something that "just happened." If one wants to find a terse, vivid, epigrammatic characterisation of something that happened in the Roman world, one naturally turns first to Gibbon. And indeed, in the excursus at the end of his 38th chapter, entitled "General observations on the Fall of the Roman empire in the West," there occurs the expressive sentence, "The stupendous fabric yielded to the pressure of its own weight." In Peter Brown's sometimes brilliant little book, *The World of Late Antiquity* (1971), there is a metaphor of a rather different kind, which equally expresses the basic idea of something that was essentially either inevitable or else fortuitous: "Altogether, the prosperity of the Mediterranean world seems to have *drained to the top*" (my italics) — Brown is speaking of the fourth century, and he has just mentioned that in the western part of the empire, in that century, the senatorial aristocracy was "five times richer, on the average, than the senators of the first century." (In the Greek East, things were not so very different, although the senatorial class was not quite so extravagantly opulent as in the West.) If I were in search of a metaphor to describe the great and growing concentration of wealth in the hands of the upper classes, I would not incline towards anything so innocent and so automatic as drainage: I should want to think in terms of something much more purposive and deliberate — perhaps the vampire bat. The burden of maintaining the imperial military and bureaucratic machine, and the Church, in addition to a leisured class consisting mainly of absentee landowners, fell primarily upon the peasantry, who formed the great bulk of the population; and, ironically enough (as I have already explained), the remarkable military and administrative reorganisation effected by a series of very able emperors from the late third century to the end of the fourth (from Diocletian and Constantine to Theodosius I) succeeded in creating an even greater number of economically "idle mouths" and thus increased the burdens upon an already overburdened peasantry. The peasants were seldom able to revolt at all, and never successfully: the imperial military machine saw to that. Only in Gaul and Spain did the Bacaudae cause serious if intermittent trouble over several generations. . . . But the merciless exploitation of the peasants made many of them receive, if not with enthusiasm at least with indifference, the barbarian invaders who might at least be expected — vainly, as it usually turned out — to shatter the oppressive imperial financial machine. Those who have been chastised with scorpions may hope for something better if they think they will be chastised only with whips.

Disharmony and Disunity

Michael Grant

The Other World Against This World

Michael Grant was born in Sweden in 1914, and was educated at Harrow and at Trinity College, Cambridge. He has been Professor of Humanity (Latin) at Edinburgh University, first Vice-Chancellor at the University of Khartoum, and President and Vice-Chancellor of the Queen's University of Belfast. Among his many publications are *From Imperium to Auctoritas, Roman Imperial Money, The World of Rome, The Climax of Rome, The Ancient Mediterranean, The Jews in the Roman World, The Army of the Caesars*, and biographies of Julius Caesar, Nero, Herod the Great, and Cleopatra.

Hundreds of reasons have been suggested for the collapse of the Roman West. Some indication of their variety can be obtained from reading Edward Gibbon's *History of the Decline and Fall of the Roman Empire*. He lists at least two dozen supposed causes of that decline and fall — military, political, economical and psychological. Many of these "causes" will be referred to in the pages that follow. But the historian himself made no attempt to marshal them one against another, or choose between them. That is rather disconcerting for the reader who is searching for quick answers. But it also shows a good deal of prudence. For an enormous, complex institution like the Roman Empire could not have been obliterated by any single, simple cause.

It was brought down by two kinds of destruction: invasions from outside, and weaknesses that arose within. The invasions are easy to identify. . . . However, they were not sufficiently formidable in themselves to have caused the Empire to perish.

Reprinted by permission of the Annenberg Press and Thomas Nelson and Sons Ltd., from Michael Grant, *The Fall of the Roman Empire: A Reappraisal* (London, 1976), pp. 19–20, 291–308.

It perished because of certain internal flaws which prevented resolute resistance to the invaders: and the greater part of this book [*The Fall of the Roman Empire: A Reappraisal*, from which this excerpt is taken] will be devoted to discovering those flaws.

I have identified thirteen defects which, in my view, combined to reduce the Roman Empire to final paralysis. They display a unifying thread: the thread of *disunity*. Each defect consists of a specific disunity which split the Empire wide apart, and thereby damaged the capacity of the Romans to meet external aggressions. Heaven forbid that we ourselves should have a monolithic society without any internal disunities at all, or any differences of character or opinion. But there can arrive a time when such differences become so irreconcilably violent that the entire structure of society is imperiled. That is what happened among the ancient Romans. And that is why Rome fell.

* * *

If the pagans, and the products of their educational system, failed to meet the challenge of the crisis owing to excessively traditional attitudes, the great churchmen and theologians, men of superior brains and character who in earlier times would have been public servants, were guilty, too often, of a different but equally serious fault: that of discouraging other people from serving the state, either in a peaceful or a warlike capacity.

This had been a natural enough attitude in the old days when the state was engaged in persecuting Christianity. Their feelings at that period were summed up by Origen: "We Christians defend the Empire by praying for it, soldiers in a spiritual welfare much more vital than any in which a Roman legionary serves." In the same spirit, his more radical contemporary Tertullian argued that a Christian soldier in the Roman army who had refused to put a garland on his head during a pagan festival was entirely justified, even though his refusal might be followed by his own imprisonment, and by the persecution of his coreligionists. Indeed, the command to "turn the other cheek," attributed to Jesus, made it difficult for a Christian to be a Roman soldier at all; and there were numerous specific instances of men who, after embracing Christianity, felt unable to serve in the army any longer.

Nor was the Christian attitude to civilian public service any more favorable. For the scriptural saying "You cannot serve two masters, God and Mammon," was interpreted by identifying Mammon with the Emperor. "Nothing, then, is more foreign to us than the state," felt Tertullian. And the church Council held in about 306 at Elvira (Illiberis) in Spain declared that no member of the faith who had been appointed to an official post could be allowed to come to church throughout his entire period of office.

But it may seem somewhat surprising that, after the Empire became Christian, the church and its leaders, although they were now the partners of the Emperor, still persisted in their old conviction that Christianity was incompatible with state service. In 313, for example, the Council of Arles in Gaul pronounced that those who wished to take up political life were excluded from communion. For, in the words of an early papal letter to the Gauls, "those who have acquired secular power and administered secular justice cannot be free from sin." In consequence, a series of Popes, including Siricius and Innocent I, debarred those who had held administrative jobs from holy orders, explaining that this was because such government posts, even if not actually sinful in themselves, were gravely perilous to a man's soul all the same.

Moreover, this veto was still specifically extended, as in earlier days, to those who had served in the army. Indeed, the Christian leaders of the time, in spite of their new and intimate associations with the government, still continued to speak out frequently and openly against military service. Athanasius explicitly praised Christianity because it alone implanted a truly pacifist disposition, since the *only* foe it battled against was Evil. Basil of Caesarea related this attitude very rigorously to practical life, declaring that a soldier who killed a man in the course of his duties was guilty of murder and must be excommunicated. Even Pope Damasus, from his position of close alliance with the state, still praised Christian soldiers who courted martyrdom by throwing away their arms. St. Martin of Tours asked to be released from the army because "I am Christ's soldier: I am not allowed to fight." And when taxed with cowardice, he was said to have offered to stand in front of the battle line armed only with a cross. But then, according to the legend, the enemy surrendered immediately, so that no such gesture proved necessary.

Paulinus, bishop of Nola, supported these arguments against the profession of arms in explicit detail, contrasting it with the wearing of armor for God.

> *Do not any longer love this world or its military service, for Scripture's authority attests that whoever is a friend of this world is an enemy of God. He who is a soldier with the sword is the servant of death, and when he sheds his own blood or that of another, this is the reward for his service.*
>
> *He will be regarded as guilty of death either because of his own death or because of his sin, because a soldier in war, fighting not so much for himself as for another, is either conquered and killed, or conquers and wins a pretext for death — for he cannot be a victor unless he first sheds blood.*

For those who were defenders of the tottering fabric of society, there is not much sign of any encouragement here. It remained for the unknown fifth-century writer *On the Calling of all Nations* to express, not merely the common belief that barbarians were the instruments of divine punishment, but the actual hope that Roman arms would *fail* against the enemy whose "weapons which destroy the world do but promote the grace of Christianity."

When such views were being expressed by bishops and theologians, it was hardly to be expected that their congregations would show any greater enthusiasm for the army and its tasks, however pressing these might be; and so the power of the Empire to resist its foes was sapped. Pacifism can only be pursued when no potential external enemies exist — and that was not the situation of ancient Rome.

Another menace to the loyal defense of the state was something more subtle. It came from Augustine, who possessed one of the best intellects of his own or any other age, and composed very numerous and abundant writings. Now Augustine could not accurately be described as a pacifist at all. The saying "turn the other cheek," he pointed out, can only be regarded as metaphorical, since to take it literally would be fatal to the welfare of the state. Wars were sometimes, he believed, a grim necessity, and might even be just, and in any case Jesus never told soldiers not to serve and fight.

Yet Augustine discouraged national service by more insidious means. Just as the monks undermined the Empire by physical withdrawal, so he undermined it, too, by a sort of spiritual withdrawal.

His work the *Civitas Dei*, rendered as the "City of God" though the word rather means "community" or "society," is not primarily a political treatise, but a work of theology. Nevertheless, its abundant pages yield important evidence of Augustine's influence on the political events of his time. Plato had described an ideal city which was the forerunner of Augustine's. It was "laid up somewhere in heaven," to be a model for actual communities upon earth. In later Greek times the Stoic philosophers had envisaged the world as a single unit, a cosmopolis, which is itself a potential City of God on earth, since all men possess a share of the divine spark. Then another philosophical thinker, Posidonius, turned this doctrine to the advantage of the Roman Empire, which he saw as the only realizable cosmopolis.

St. Paul, too, wrote that the minds of the enemies of Christ are set on earthly things, whereas Christian believers on earth "by contrast are citizens of heaven." Yet he held that earthly governments had to be obeyed, for they are instituted by God and are in the service of God, so that those who rebel against them are flouting divine authority. And in the same spirit the Gospels record a much-discussed saying of Jesus, "Render to Caesar the things that are Caesar's, and to God the things that are God's."

After the accession of Constantine, it was believed by his supporters that the words of Jesus and Paul enjoining obedience to the earthly power had become peculiarly relevant, since the unity between the heavenly and earthly communities detected by Posidonius had actually begun, under the reigning Emperor's auspices, to come about. Subsequently Theodosius I, by his total union between state and church, seemed to have completed the process, and the official doctrine was now insistent that by serving the Christian government a man was also serving heaven.

But when Alaric sacked Rome in 410, a wave of pessimism came over the relations between church and state. This gloom was based on certain antique attitudes. In particular there had always been a widespread pagan doctrine that the world, so far from exhibiting modern concepts of progress, was steadily declining from the Golden Age of the past down to the Iron Age of the present, with catastrophe to come in the future. Such doctrines, which conveniently coincided with Christian views of the Day of Doom and the Last Judgment, enabled Ambrose, for example, to take a most unfavorable view of the condition and prospects of the Roman Empire. After the battle of Adrianople, he announced "the massacre of all humanity, the end of the world," and then again in 386 he recorded "diseases spreading, time nearing its end. We are indeed in the twilight of the world." Christianity he saw as the crop coming just before the frosts of the winter: and the approaching world's end, as one of his followers explicitly declared, was to be preceded by the collapse of Rome.

Since the Romans, when they expressed over-optimism, were speaking foolishly, it seems hypercritical to denounce them when they were pessimistic as well. And, indeed, there was one thing to be said in favor of this gloomier attitude. It did at least appreciate that there was something terribly wrong. But useful plans to put it right were scarcely more apparent among Christians than among pagans.

Upon this world of unconstructive thinking burst Alaric in 410. Almost a century earlier, the Christian writer Lactantius had said that the fall of the city of Rome would mean the end of the world, and now, with Alaric's onslaught, both these events seemed to have come at one and the same time. "Eleven hundred and sixty-three years after the foundation of Rome," declared Gibbon, "the imperial city, which had subdued and civilized so considerable a part of mankind, was delivered to the licentious fury of the tribes of Germany and Scythia." Although, in fact, the Visigoths only stayed for three days, and did not do as much damage as might have been expected, this blow that felled the Eternal City seemed an appalling horror to optimists and pessimists alike.

Jerome, although far away in Bethlehem, took it as hard as anyone else. Alaric's earlier invasions had already filled him with the gloomiest forebodings, and now, after the sack of the city, he wrote to other friends in desperation, almost believing that the blackest prophecies had been right, and that the last days of the world were truly come.

> *I dare hardly speak until I receive more definite news. For I am torn between hope and despair, tormented by the terrible things that have befallen our friends. But now that this glorious Light of the World has been tampered with — defiled; and now that, with this city, the whole world, so to speak, is faced with annihilation, "I am dumb, and am humbled, and kept silent from good things."*

Three years later, he was still reverting to the same theme.

> *Terrifying news comes to us from the West. Rome has been taken by assault. Men are ransoming their lives with gold. Though despoiled,*

> *they are still hounded, so that after their goods they may pay with their very lives.*
>
> *My voice is still, and sobs disturb my every utterance. The city has been conquered which had once subjugated an entire world.*

Nevertheless, the Christian view remained equivocal since Alaric, in his work of destruction, seemed to be acting as the human instrument of God, and imposing a divine visitation, punishment, and test. "God's providence," wrote Augustine, "constantly uses war to correct and chasten the corrupt morals of mankind, as it also uses such afflictions to train men in a righteous and laudable way of life, removing to a better state those whose life is approved, or else keeping them in this world for further service."

Yet on hearing for the first time of the capture of Rome Augustine's first reaction, like Jerome's, had been one of deep shock. "Tidings of terror are reaching us," he declared to his African congregation. "There has been a massacre: also great fires, looting, murder, torture." Later he realized that these first reports were overstated. Acting with relative restraint, Alaric, himself a Christian, had spared the personnel and property of the church.

However, many people, and not only pagans, were asking why, since the Imperial government was Christian and allegedly enjoyed God's backing, had God allowed such a thing to happen. Nothing so frightful had ever occurred under pagan rule. It was in order to meet this challenge that Augustine began to write the twenty-two books of the *City of God*. "The first five," explains its author, "refute those who attribute prosperity and adversity to the cult of pagan gods or to the prohibition of this cult. The next five are against those who hold that ills are never wanting to men, but that worship of the pagan gods helps towards the future life after death." The second part of the work contains twelve books. The first four describe the birth of the two cities, one of God, the other of the world. The second four continue their story, and the third four depict their final destiny. These last twelve books contain a far-reaching philosophy of history which does not depend solely on Alaric's capture of Rome but possesses a universal application.

Augustine had read Plato's *Republic* in Latin translations, and had studied commentaries on the work. But he borrowed the concept of the two cities from certain contemporary North African Christians, the

Donastists . . . who held that one city served God and his loyal angels, while the other worked for the Devil and his rebel angels and demons. At present, it was true, the two cities seemed inextricably mixed together within the church as in the rest of the world, but at the Last Judgment they would appear in manifest separation, one on God's left and the other on his right, like the captor city Babylon and its liberated captive Jerusalem.

This vision of captivity and liberation excited Augustine and inspired him. And in consequence, during the years following 410, he began to develop this whole theme for his readers and congregations, elaborating it with the passion of a masterly and persuasive artist.

Two loves, he says, have created two cities: love of God the heavenly city, to the contempt of self; love of self the earthly city, to the contempt of God. The city of God is the city of the righteous, which contains God and his angels and saints in heaven, and all men and women who lead good lives on earth. The earthly city contains all unrighteous men and women wherever they be in the universe — fallen angels, the souls of the unrighteous, the unrighteous in the world. Although, therefore, marginal points of contact exist, the earthly city is *not the same* as the Roman Empire.

What, then, does Augustine think of that Empire? The answer is founded on his doctrine of Grace. Without the god-given help to human beings, he feels that we who are lumps of perdition — sinful ever since Adam's Fall — can never attain eternal salvation. Augustine's own recurrent struggles between the flesh and the spirit caused him to share St. Paul's poor opinion of what a person can achieve by his own unaided will, and made him break with the more optimistic, classical, humanistic view that we can achieve great things by our own endeavors.

Augustine's attitude incurred the intense disapproval and anger of another Christian theologian of the day. This was Pelagius. Of British or Irish extraction, he came to Rome as a monk about 400. Like others, he was horrified by Alaric's sack of Rome, when "the mistress of the world shivered, crushed with fear, at the sound of the blaring trumpets and the howling of the Goths."

But Pelagius's reaction to such disasters was by no means limited to fatalistic gloom and despair. Both before and after the capture of the city, he found himself deeply dissatisfied with the moral sluggishness of many prosperous people of Rome. In an attempt to raise their easygoing standards, he insisted on a strenuous individual endeavor to attain salvation. He was convinced that the barrier of corruption which keeps original innocence and goodness out of our reach is insubstantial, and can be overcome by a bracing effort: we sin by a *voluntary* imitation of Adam, and an equally voluntary decision can cast our sins behind us.

The salvation to which Pelagius primarily referred was not of this world. Yet his doctrine was obviously applicable to worldly salvation as well — to the rehabilitation of the failing Roman Empire. If people bestirred themselves more and tried harder, it could be deduced from Pelagius, they would be better men. And that also meant, though he did not put it in such a way, that they would be better able to come to the rescue of their country.

This earnest belief in self-help caused him to abhor the tenth book of Augustine's *Confessions*, in which the writer repeatedly emphasized his dependence not on his own will but on the Grace of God. Pelagius himself, on the other hand, while not disbelieving in God's Grace, failed to see it as an overriding necessity. To him it was rather a form of divine assistance which can derive from moral exhortation and from a study of the supreme example of Christ: Grace, in this sense, will help us to fulfill and express the noble natures that have been bestowed on us by God. Like the earlier sort of modern existentialists before they became closely aligned with Marxism, Pelagius believed that man makes his own history on his own account.

Learning of this insistence upon the basic soundness and effectiveness of the human will, Augustine revolted against Pelagius even more violently than Pelagius had revolted against Augustine. He accused Pelagius of teaching, "like the philosophers of the pagans," that man by his own unassisted free will could achieve goodness without any help from God at all. Probably the criticism was unjustified, since what Pelagius really wanted to say was that heaven helps those who help themselves. But Augustine persisted in his censures for many years and wrote a treatise, *On Free Will*, endeavoring to strike what he felt to be a more pious balance between men's limited capacity for autonomous enterprise and his dependence on the divine power. In effect, however, the "higher freedom" which emerged, while professing to admit the liberty of the will, tended towards its annihilation as a well-spring of action.

Although Augustine's diffidence in his own powers (reflected in this formulation) displays an engaging humility, the doctrine of Pelagius was of greater value — on the practical plane of daily events and emergencies — to the later Roman Empire. It is true that he disliked the current spiritual inertia, and perhaps the whole social system that lay behind it, so much that he even spoke warmly in favor of monasticism. Nevertheless, his doctrine of the will at least wanted people to *try*. Augustine's philosophy, on the other hand, led to fatalism. Yet his incomparable eloquence, ably supported by many other preachers, ensured that it was his view which ultimately prevailed.

So Pelagius was doomed to failure. Jerome called him a fat hound weighed down by Scotch porridge, and he twice suffered excommunication. When and where he died is unknown. But after his death, the controversy continued with unabated vigor, and Gallic monks and theologians felt considerable sympathy with his views, for Augustine's increasingly vehement assertions of Grace as man's only hope seemed to undermine human effort.

Indeed, his pronouncements also carried more fundamental political implications, affecting the whole concept of the Roman Empire. For since man, he concluded, is so totally corrupted by the fall of Adam that he is bound at some time to sin, and even Grace cannot prevent this inevitable outcome; since, that is to say, for as long as he lives, he can never cease to be flawed, then all his institutions are flawed as well. Even the church, though it provides the only bridge to the heavenly city, remains a mixture of good wheat and bad weeds. How much more imperfect, then, must be the state, the Roman Empire itself!

True, although often perverted by evil wills, it is a natural and a divine necessity which God granted to the Romans. By his ordinance, continued Augustine, there is a king for temporal life, as there is a king for eternal life. Earthly rulers have special services they can render to God, just because they are rulers. And although Constantine was by no means perfect — for Augustine was one of those who believed that Christianity had lost virtue as it gained wealth and power — he paid honor to Theodosius I, as a prince whose devotion to the faith was exemplary.

When such men rule, one can see "a faint shadowy resemblance between the Roman Empire and the heavenly city." The state, in fact, has its uses. Love of our neighbor, felt Augustine, makes our patriotic and civic duties obligatory. Soldiers, rulers, and judges alike have to stay at their posts. And yet, all the same, we are reading the thoughts of a man in whom national feeling is so strictly and totally subordinated to religious considerations that it can hardly, in any meaningful sense, be said to exist. From the nationalist sentiments which had defended the frontiers of ancient Rome for so many centuries we have traveled a vast distance. For example, while granting that wars can be just and even necessary, Augustine concludes that their "victories bring death with them or are doomed to death," and the vast extent of Rome's Empire, he adds, has given rise to every sort of detestable foreign and civil war. Augustine even says he would have preferred a number of small nations living in peace to the monolithic Empire of the Romans. "Without justice," he declares, "governments are merely great bands of brigands" — gangsterism on a massive scale. But "without justice" is precisely what, in the very nature of things, these states inevitably were: and what Rome could not fail to be.

And so he preached, as others had preached before him, that "we do not want to have dealings with the powers that be." That is frank: it is a call to withhold service from the government. Equally frank is his reminder that the Empire is bound to collapse anyway. "If heaven and earth are to pass away, why is it surprising if at some time the state is going to come to a stop? — if what God has made will one day vanish, then surely what Romulus made will disappear much sooner." Even the current identification of church and state will not, cannot, suffice to stop the rot.

Where does all this leave the individual citizen? Rome, for his benefit, has been firmly cut down to size. Our *real*, permanent fatherland, he is told — the only true kingdom, according to the strictest idea of what is right — is elsewhere altogether. "What we want," states Augustine, "is a way to help us to return to *that* kingdom: that is how we shall bring our sorrows to an end." As for all the earthly crises and catastrophes, they can just be ignored — or even welcomed, seeing that God has sent them as a discipline. The calamities of a country in which you are merely a foreigner do not really affect your interests at all. When, therefore, such calamities appear, just treat them as an invitation to concentrate your desires on things eternal: and rejoice that your treasure is in a place where no enemy has the power to approach. To a patriotic pagan, disturbed by the disasters that have befallen

Rome, Augustine spells out the message: "Please pardon us if *our* country, up above, has to cause trouble to yours . . . you would acquire still greater merit if you served a higher fatherland."

Those are not words that will impel a man to the defense of the falling Roman Empire. Augustine has shifted the center of gravity so that the state is now a good deal less than half of what matters: far from helping his country to survive, his attitude contributed to its downfall.

His implied suggestion that, since it was up to Providence whether the Roman world should collapse or not, human endeavor could do nothing about it in any case, met with the strong disapproval not only presumably of Pelagius, but of Gibbon. For the task Gibbon set himself was to show that it was not God's Providence but very real, earthly enemies and causes which destroyed the Romans: that "man is not trapped by history," as David P. Jordan puts it in his book *Gibbon and His Roman Empire*; "he does not live in a haunted house, he can emancipate himself through reason."

Although Augustine's full influence was not exerted for generations to come, subsequent writers during the last years of the Western Roman Empire were already echoing his fatalistic attitude. For example, it was perhaps now that the poet Commodianus positively gloated over the downfall of the city: "She who bragged that she was eternal now weeps to eternity." And in the words of Orientius, bishop of Auch in southwest France, "why go over the funeral ceremonies of a world falling into ruins, in accordance with the common law of all that passes away?" Moreover, Orosius, whom Augustine commissioned to write a history of Rome, not only reminds us once again that Rome deserved the German onslaughts — because in earlier days it had persecuted the Christians — but that these attacks will actually be beneficial, "although this may involve the crumbling of our Empire." Presbyter Salvian, who believed the same, added two realistic comments. First, the Empire was *already* dead, or breathing its last. Secondly, most Romans lacked the imagination to realize the supreme peril they were in: and if they did happen to possess such discernment, they lacked the nerve to do anything about it.

For the existence of this inertia — which is a very accurate diagnosis — the suggestion of Augustine that human endeavor could be of no consequence, either in this situation or any other, bore a share of the blame; or at least he very accurately represented a prevailing feeling. "Help from without," declared the zealous Samuel Smiles, author of that nineteenth-century gospel of work called *Self-Help*, "is often enfeebling in its effects, but help from within invariably invigorates." Help from within was precisely what neither the pagan nor Christian ethics of the later Roman Empire were able to provide: and the characteristic ideas of both faiths fell all too readily into line with the numerous other tendencies conspiring to bring about Rome's fall.

St. Augustine

Defense of the Christians

Aurelius Augustinus (St. Augustine, A.D. 354–430) was a Roman citizen born in Algeria where he later became Bishop of Hippo Regius, an important Roman city of that region. When the Visigoths under Alaric captured and sacked Rome in 410, pagan Romans blamed the Christians for the calamity. One of Augustine's purposes in writing his great work, *The City of God*, was to refute these charges.

If man's sickly understanding would not set plain truth at defiance, but humbly submit this common infirmity to the tonic of wholesome doctrine until, by filial trust in God's help, it regained its strength, those who think straight and express their thoughts in well-chosen speech would have no need of many words to correct the errors of baseless assumption. Unfortunately, however, there prevails a major and malignant malady of fools, the victims of which mistake their irrational impulses for truth and reason, even when confronted with as much evidence as any man has a right to expect from another. It may be an excess of blindness which prevents them from seeing the most glaring facts, or a perverse obstinacy which prevents them from accepting the facts when seen. This compels me to present more diffusely, not for

From St. Augustine, *The City of God*, an abridged version from the translation by G.G. Walsh, S.J., D.B. Zema, S.J., G. Monahan, O.S.U., and D.J. Honan, edited by Vernon J. Bourke, Doubleday, 1958. Reprinted by permission of Doubleday & Company Inc.

their closed eyes to see, but, so to speak, for their hands to touch and feel, some obvious points.

Yet, if we always felt obliged to reply to counterstatements, when would there be an end to the argument or a limit to discussion? For, those who cannot grasp what is said, or, if they understand the truth, are too obdurate to accept it, keep on replying and, according to Holy Writ, "speak iniquity" and never weary of empty words. You can easily see what an endless, wearisome, and fruitless task it would be, if I were to refute all the unconsidered objections of people who pigheadedly contradict everything I say.

And so, my dear Marcellinus, I hope that neither you nor any others, for whose profit and pleasure this work is offered in the love of Christ, will read what I write in the spirit of men who demand an answer every time they hear any objections and act like those silly women whom St. Paul describes as "ever learning and never attaining to the knowledge of the truth."

When I began in the previous Book to speak of the City of God — which moved me to undertake, with God's help, this entire work — my first plan was to challenge the view of those who hold that the Christian religion is responsible for all the wars desolating this miserable world and, in particular, for the recent barbarian sack of the City of Rome. It is true that the Christian religion forbids pagans to honor demons with unspeakable sacrifices; but, as I pointed out, they should thank Christ for the boon that, out of regard for His Name and in disregard of the traditional usages of war, the barbarians gave them immunity in spacious Christian buildings. What is more, they treated both the genuine followers of Christ and many who through fear pretended to be such with great concern. They refused to take measures against them which the laws of war permitted.

Thence arose the question: Why did God, on the one hand, bestow His good things upon the impious and the thankless, while, on the other, the enemy's hard blows fell with equal weight upon the good and the wicked alike? In order to answer this all-embracing question as fully as the scope of my work demanded, I lingered on it for various reasons. First, because many are disturbed in mind when they observe how, in the daily round of life, God's gifts and man's brutalities oftentimes fall indifferently and indiscriminately to the lot of both the good and the bad; but, above all, because I wanted to offer to those pure and holy women whose modesty had been outraged by the barbarian soldiery, but whose purity of soul had stood adamant, the consoling assurance that they have no reason to bewail their lives, since there is no personal guilt for them to bewail.

* * *

Why, then, do not you Romans with your noble character, you sons of the Reguli, Scaevolae, Scipii, and Fabricii, let your hearts go out to these better things. Look at the difference between these things and the base arrogance and deceiving wickedness of the demons. However great and good your natural gifts may be, it takes true piety to make them pure and perfect; with impiety, they merely end in loss and pain. Choose now your course, not to seek glory in yourself, but to find it infallibly in the true God. At one time, you could enjoy the applause of your people, but by God's mysterious providence the true religion was not there for you to choose.

But, it is now day; awake as you awoke in the persons of those men in whose sterling virtue and sufferings for the faith we glory. They battled on all sides against hostile powers and, conquering by their fearless death, "have purchased this country for us with their blood." To this Country we pleadingly invite you. Join its citizens, for it offers more than mere sanctuary, it offers the true remission of your sins.

Give no heed to the degenerate progeny who blame Christ and Christians for what they call bad times, and long for times which assure them, not a peaceful life, but undisturbed wickedness. Such times were never to your liking, not even for an earthly fatherland. Reach out now for the heavenly country. You will have very little to suffer for it, and in it you will reign in very truth, and forever. In that land there is no Vestal altar, no statue of Jupiter on the Capitol, but the one true God, who "will not limit you in space or time, but will give an empire universal and eternal." Seek no false and lying gods; rather, cast them from you with scorn and shine forth in true freedom. They are not gods, but fiendish spirits, to whom your eternal happiness is a torment.

Never did Juno so intensely begrudge the Trojans, your ancestors in the flesh, the battlements of Rome, as do those demons, whom you still fancy to be gods, begrudge an everlasting home to the whole human race.

You have already, in part, passed judgment on these spirits, for, while you placated them with stage plays, you branded with infamy the actors who performed them. Let your freedom assert its rights against the unclean spirits who have placed upon you the obligation of solemnly exhibiting their shame as though it were a holy thing.

You took civic rights away from performers of Olympian scandals. Now, beseech the true God to take away from you those gods who delight in immoralities — in lust, if the sins are facts; in lying, if they are feigned. You did well to ostracize the mimes and mummers from civil society. Keep a sharper watch now. Divine majesty is in no way appeased by arts which dishonor man's dignity. How, then, can you place in the ranks of the holy powers of heaven gods who delight in homage so unclean, while you banned from the lowest ranks of Roman citizens the men who enacted such homage?

Glorious beyond compare is the heavenly city. There, victory is truth, dignity is holiness, peace is happiness, life is eternity. If you blushed to tolerate that sort of men among your citizens, how much less will the heavenly city tolerate that sort of gods? Wherefore, if you long to reach that blessed country, shun the company of demons. Gods who are propitiated by infamous rites are unworthy of the worship of decent men. Deny religious rites to the gods, by a Christian reform, just as you denied civil dignity to the actors, by the censor's decree.

As regards earthly happiness and physical evils which alone the wicked wish to enjoy or refuse to endure, I shall show in the sequel that not even over these have those demons the control people imagine. Indeed, even if they did have, then we should scorn those things rather than, for their sake, worship those gods and so fail to attain the blessings they begrudge us. However, not even over those things have demons the power attributed to them by those who maintain that they must on that account be propitiated. But, as I said, more of this later. Here, I bring this Book to a close.

Ramsay MacMullen

Militarism in the Late Empire

Ramsay MacMullen was born in New York City in 1928 and educated at Harvard University. He has taught at the University of Oregon and Brandeis University, and since 1967 has been Professor of History and Classics at Yale University. In addition to the works whose excerpts are included here, he has written several important studies of social history in the later Roman Empire, including *Roman Social Relations, 50* B.C. *to* A.D. *284* and *Roman Governments' Response to Crisis,* A.D. *285–337.*

The Roman army, being used for ends not strictly military, lost its professional edge in a process stretching over perhaps two centuries, first accelerated by Septimius Severus and never reversed thereafter. Partly as a result, but more because of the violence of the later Empire, civilians had to arm themselves for their own protection. Civilian turned soldier, soldier turned civilian, in a *rapprochement* to a middle ground of waste and confusion. By the process, each influenced the other, but one direction of influence, the militarization of civilians, was particularly significant, and did much to change society. Such in sum is what this book [*Soldier and Civilian in the Later Roman Empire*] tries to prove.

A comparison of Rome's military effectiveness at the start and at the end of the Empire is instructive, and depressing. In a battle of five thousand legionaries against as many enemies, a spectator in Augustus's day would have had to give heavy odds on the Romans. Man for man, in physical strength and courage, Romans may have been no better than, say, the Gauls (whom Caeser eagerly enrolled); even in armament, their shields were to cumbersome, their swords too short, and their *pilum* something of an antique, and these in time were all improved or discarded. Still, they won their battles, by everything that distinguishes an army from militia: habits of command and obedience, morale, a superb supply system, and much else. That same spectator, however, four centuries later, would have found it a very even struggle between Romans and Huns, or Romans and Parthians. A Roman victory had become — such is the impression one has, from the accounts of the time — a mere fifty-fifty proposition.

The fault of the army lay not in its size. There were more troops under arms — or at least on the rolls — in 350 than ever before. Half or more of them were of the kind that Vegetius (1.3) so nostalgically endorses, country folk "ignorant of the baths, careless of luxuries, simple in mind, content with little." Such were, such rather should have been, the *limitanei*, encouraged by the additional consciousness that it was their own farms and houses that they guarded. Yet the *limitanei* were clearly looked on as second-class troops. Synesius is contemptuous of those in Cyrenaica, while the system of defense dependent on them alone, in one broad area of Tripolitania, collapsed after the middle of the fourth century. More might perhaps have been expected of the city troops. But Ammianus's account of the useless garrison at Autun, which required the support of veteran volunteers, is confirmed by Count Ursulus's somber apostrophe, as he surveyed the ruins of Amida: "Behold the spirit with which the soldiers defend our cities! These are the men for whose high wages the imperial treasury is exhausted."

Of the two kinds of soldier most numerous and typical in Ursulus's day, *limitanei* spent most of their time on their little estates, and, being as far as we know never drilled, taken on maneuvers, nor subjected to any regular discipline, they fought as we would expect, like amateurs. This is not to say that they were all farmers. If we may judge from the signs they have left, especially in Africa, they formed a shabby squirarchy in the frontier zones, semibarbarous, semisoldier, in forts that looked like houses. Their urban equivalents proved equally, but differently, inadequate. To them were entrusted, from the mid-third century, the cities newly walled and generally reduced in area; and here garrisons fell prey to diversions that Vegetius condemns: *balnea*, *deliciae*, and the rest. What is missing, of course, is something between farm life and city life, that is, the camp of the Antonine army.

That camp was never typical of troop emplacements in the East, where urban quarters notoriously prevailed, and in the West it was, after Diocletian, less and less built either for an army on the march or for a permanent post. Existing camps were abandoned, their shells left to pillage or to civilian squatters, or, with a fireplace in the antechapel, a latrine in the adjutant's office, children's sandals in the barracks, and sleeping quarters in the storehouses, they were remodeled to accommodate married men and their families. In some were included facilities — pens, troughs, stables — for domestic animals driven to refuge by the peasants round about. The most conspicuous achievement of Roman military engineers, Hadrian's Wall, being damaged in the raids of the 360s, was indeed soon repaired, but by efforts described as "clumsy botching."

When the army flourished, as under Hadrian, its habits remained reasonably pure. The largest contingents were forbidden to own farms outside or gardens inside the camp, "for fear that through the desire of cultivating the soil they may be withdrawn from military service." Off-duty guilds were banned as well as part-time trading and legal marriages. If troops had to be stationed in a city, they were divided from their hosts by an interior crosswall, suggesting at least a theory of separation, whatever the facts may have been. Septimius Severus, however, introduced very different policies: legitimate marriage for serving soldiers, permission to indulge in trade and usury, off-duty clubs for lower officers; or arrangements for swifter promotion, and for military careers borrowing greater brilliance from posts once reserved for senators. One can even see a lowering of the barriers between soldiers and civilians: liberal grants of municipal or colonial status to camp settlements, barracks abandoned or troops removed from camps into cities, as at Alexandria under Caracalla. It is not likely that these measures were the rash payment of political promises. The army was indeed the dynasty's chief support. It was also the only bulwark against the barbarians. And there were sober advisers able to deter Septimius, had he attempted to strengthen himself by weakening the empire in a merely selfish purchase of army loyalty. The emperor's council was, as a matter of fact, especially brilliant, and must have included several authors of treatises *de re militari*. What, then, can explain the deliberate tendency of the whole Severan family to soften the edge of military discipline?

The reason for the change most often given is the one just glanced at, the political needs of the Severi. Though much evidence supports this explanation, there is another fact that should be kept in mind, the difficulty of recruiting. Against the Marcomanni, Marcus Aurelius had armed slaves, against the Costoboci, Boeotian volunteers, against the Parthians, Spartan *symmachoi* and the *diogmitai* of townships and of private citizens. His son abandoned war, and raised legionary pay 25 percent. That was not enough. To keep pace with recent prices, Commodus should have managed an increase, not from 300 to 375 denarii, but to 800. Even the dramatic doubling of pay within the first twenty years of the Severi was inadequate. It had to be supplemented by those relaxations of discipline just described in order to make the service more attractive.

It should be remembered, too, how inflexible the Roman exchequer proved in any financial crisis. Emperors lived almost from hand to mouth, and any irregular expense had to be met by expedients — really, considering the grandeur and complexity of the empire, they are extraordinary — such as the invention of petty taxes, debasement of coinage, auction of the palace furniture, or, under a facade of political revenge, the harrying of the rich out of their properties. To the last, Septimius turned with enthusiasm. Even so, an increase of 100 percent in legionary pay, in his and his son's reigns, must have meant a permanent increase of 25 percent in the budget as a whole. The military and financial policies of the Severi must have reduced them to extremities.

There is nothing like bankruptcy to change a man's views. We cannot accuse Septimius of being naturally lax in his treatment of the army (later emperors confirmed the course he took), nor can we ascribe his policies to nothing but the payment of political debts. He and his advisers seem to have made a sober, fixed decision about the army which implied its general inadequacy, and which involved a major revision of the amount and mode of its payment, the conditions of its service, and the relations which must henceforth exist between it and its commander in chief. That this decision was based on economic considerations can be shown fully enough in the various attempts to make the army self-supporting, for example in the use of camp territories to supply their own troops with bread and meat. The evidence for the lease of legionary lands to soldiers, for the existence of legionary herds (attested by *pecuarii*), for soldiers engaging in businesses of their own and (under Alexander) for precursors of the later *limitanei* on a very large scale, all is predominantly or wholly Severan. If we look into other army needs — bricks, timber, arms — we are again met by Severan innovations, taking the the form of factories in the West staffed and supervised by soldiers, covering acres and acres, firmly housed in stone buildings or in earthwork mills, and capable of a most impressive output. The object, autarky, is written large in these interesting experiments, some of which, such as legionary sawmills, apparently failed, others of which proved their value in a long history. Legionary bricks were sold in quantity to private individuals in the neighborhood well into the fourth century. Arms factories still existed in the fifth, managed by officers taken from the army. There were nearly fifty of them, spread throughout the North and East.

Autarky may have been a key word in the councils of the Severi. It was given to the army; it fitted the sweeping proscriptions of Septimius's enemies, by which he assembled such unprecedented crown domains; and the two together, army and crown estates, can be seen at work in a wide area in Africa, where new lands were reclaimed for agriculture and old lands defended by the cooperation of soldiers and *coloni*. Within the whole complex of imperial obligations, the army could play a further part. It could be used for building in the provinces, as had been done before, but as became more frequent in the late second and third centuries. It could be used in administration. A study of soldiers detached to the offices of civil magistrates, under such titles as *beneficiarii consularis*, shows a striking increase under Septimius which saved the cost of the freedmen and slaves used earlier. At the same time there is evidence for a very sharp increase in the use of centurions for police work in Egypt, and for *stationarii* as judges and tax collectors elsewhere.

These miscellaneous activities undoubtedly worked their effects on the men involved. Many, for their full twenty-five years, did nothing but write; many attended magistrates as messengers, ushers, confidential agents, and accountants, measuring their promotion from chair to chair, from office to office. It was surely impossible to withdraw such clerks to active service. Even within the legions, from Septimius's day, new duties made necessary new nonmilitary ranks — *actuarii, codicillarii, scribae* — and camp facilities for office work are fuller. When we add the police work of the soldier who "served nineteen years as guard" on an imperial estate, the specialization of the "camp nailsmith," or the pride of another who displayed on his tombstone only an engineer's compass and square, we have a total of very diverse, but certainly not very military, activities. They grew more and more common. From a mass of evidence, some fragments are especially striking: that a fourth-century writer could speak of "the soldiers who *usually* levied the taxes"; that a tax could become known simply as "the *primipilus*"; that a police force could be called "the Centurionics." Everyday speech is often revealing.

Two illustrations will be enough to show how involved the army might become in duties not properly its own. Both can be completely documented. We may take first the Egyptian end of the *annona civica*. A peasant sees at harvest time the tax collector attended by a soldier, who is present if necessary to enforce payment. So many bags of grain are handed over, taken by oxcart to a wharf (built by soldiers) on the Nile, and there put on board a barge. One or more soldiers go along as guards, and their expenses — wine, presumably, and food — are covered by a special tax paid upon lading. The grain is stored in the granaries of Alexandria, supervised by more soldiers; transported to Rome by a guild of shippers whose patron is a soldier; and checked at the capital by a *b(ene)f(iciarius) proc. Aug. annon.* and a *subcenturio*.

Or we may take, over a longer span of time, some hypothetical colony. Soldiers, needless to say, have conquered the land for Rome. They mark its extent with boundary posts, it is they who divide its territory into strips along a grid, and they trace its walls and its chief streets crossing at a forum. They supervise allotments and the tax status of each plot. The overall shape of the town is that of a camp. Some of them, as veterans, settle down in the richer sections, attract more of their kind, dominate the senate, and fill the town's magistracies. They fill, too, the reserved seats in its amphitheater (built by their subscriptions), enjoying a prominence merited by their wealth, their influence, and by the generosity they have displayed in a score of public monuments. From the town's birth to its maturity, soldiers have supplied the forming force. If, in the third century, it is attacked, soldiers again — not a garrison alone, but veterans who volunteer — will defend it.

Two other illustrations may serve for the reverse purpose, to show the approximation of civilians to soldiers. The most unlikely place to look is the Church. Yet in Antioch and Alexandria it had its own troops, on the eastern border it had "an army of monks" in turreted monasteries; a bishop and his deacon led the defense of Cyrene, and watched two brother bishops dispute the possession of an abandoned fortlet. In Cyrenaica the fortified church, in Numidia and Tripolitania the fortified church-storehouse, were common features; and throughout Africa and the East, religious strife invited churchmen to work hand in glove with the army, "raging around in company with Dukes and

Counts," as the Council of Sardica said of Athanasius. If we look next at the city of the late Empire, we see it too, in desperate suddenness, building its fortifications out of pillars and tombstones, incorporating any great structure like a basilica or an amphitheater into its defenses, walling in an abandoned camp or walling out its very forum, and calling upon its youth and its veterans to form themselves into an army. Everything was done to make a city, in its gates, towers, and perimeter, resemble a fort, and if necessary an army engineer was called in to produce a more perfect transformation.

But this transformation is often too perfect. Ambiguous pictures of fourth-century *enceintes* in the manuscripts of the *Notitia Dignitatum* or in the mosaic of Orbe cannot be identified for certain as *civitates* or *castella*; clay models of a gate may belong to a city or a camp; the *castellum* and monastery, like the *centenaria* and fortified farms, are even to the eye of the expert literally indistinguishable. It cannot be known whether the Libyan *tribuni* of the fourth century are or are not in the army proper, or whether a bishop who is described as formerly *strateusamenos* was "serving" as a civilian or military "soldier." His services were in either case a *militia*.

One need not swallow Herbert Spencer entire to see, in this loss of specialization, in this slurring of the division between the professions of war and peace, a very serious degeneracy. Obviously a soldier who had a farm to look after, with tenants and flocks, or one who spent long terms of duty in an arms factory or at a grain depot, could not do his own job properly. A provincial senator called upon to organize a militia, to stand watches on the walls, or to improvise shelter for refugee peasants, was, just as clearly, not serving the normal purposes for which cities are assembled. These were the sins of omission, so to speak — specialization neglected. There was also the sin of commission, the intrusion of a man of one profession into another man's. It can be illustrated best for the soldier, who enjoyed great prestige throughout our period and encroached aggressively on civilian institutions. That this was utterly baneful no one today need be reminded. A Europe that has returned, in recent times, by route of brown and black shirts, to the medieval customs of livery and maintenance, has shown what happens when soldiers enter politics. The Roman equivalent was military patronage. Its growth can be traced easily and naturally in a number of fairly long and informative inscriptions of the third century that show officers as saviors in time of attack, and as temporary overseers of almost every aspect of local government. When to their legitimate position was added an estate in the country, wealth, blood ties with the local aristocracy, and the popularity of a benefactor, the military patron was almost complete. The only thing still to be mentioned was control of armed men, and that of course was always available to him. At the same time, the civil official was beginning to encroach on local government. He too was chosen more and more as municipal patron, he too was found concentrating his rich houses in the best parts of town, active on the side in usury and trade, and exacting from his lowly clients "great sacks of beans with which to sow his private acres." The private citizen, a magnate indeed but without imperial office, exercised *his* patronage by suborning troops and secret police from the state, or by arming his servants. These, however, are rather a feature of the fifth century. Under the name of *bucellarii* they are known in detail in Egypt. From three directions — soldier, civil servant, and private civilian — the armed patron emerges.

It is Septimius Severus who did the most to turn troops into odd-job men. His motives seem to have been mainly fiscal. A complete loss of specialization among soldiers is represented two centuries later by the commander of frontier guards. It is possible to imagine him owning some local fields in his private capacity, supervising the tenants of others officially, a man of standing on the countryside, living in his own fortified mansion, and, with his servants — some troops, some slaves or *coloni* — able to press his own olives, guard his own house from attack, or fend off the tax collector. He may appear as the logical end of the Severan policies. Yet where the captain of the village is so nearly approached from other directions, the explanation for his rise must be a much broader one, concerning itself with the empire as a whole. Material for this explanation, well known, may be left to the general histories: unrest, fiscal oppression, barbarian invasions. The story of the Roman army is part of the story of the empire. Like that story, too, it is told slowly. The sluggish pace of change, traced here over some two hundred years, must be emphasized yet again. It is unlikely that contemporaries were even aware of its direction, however keenly they felt its results.

So much for the "*rapprochement* to a middle ground of waste and confusion." But it is also argued that only on this ground could soldier and civilian exchange the habits of life peculiar to each.

Civilian influence on the army is not easy to detect. In one broad sense it was complete, that is, the majority of the late fourth-century army was a mere militia. Its roots were in civilian life, rural or urban. More narrowly, the soldier as a soldier was little changed, indeed could not have been, short of fighting with a scythe in his hand or giving the orders of the day in hexameters. Some "civilianizing" may be seen in the architecture of the *praetorium*, which in the early Empire was already borrowing the general plan and inner comforts of a private villa. Another instance of the same process was the adaptation of parts of the camp to ceremonial purposes, and ultimately to worship. High officers did fight, or communicate with their men in their proper capacity, differently in the fourth century than they had done in the first. But the sum of all this is not very significant.

On the other hand, the influence of the army on civil institutions was profound. While the military way of doing things was perhaps no better than any other, it was supported by the marked favor of the emperor, from Septimius Severus on; in remote areas, it represented all that was visible of Rome's victorious civilization; and when brigands and barbarians descended on the helpless calm of the inner empire, the soldier took on the aura of a deliverer. He led the local defense, he mobilized arms, men, and money. He concentrated civil authority in his hands, at first quite unofficially, but more and more with the sanction of the state. Finally, he and his works were ubiquitous. Four of the preceding chapters [of *Soldier and Civilian*] have been devoted to proving just that, and what they have tried to emphasize is the steadily increasing physical closeness of soldier to civilian. Not only were camps largely abandoned (if they did not turn into cities themselves), but garrisons were fixed in a larger number of cities. On the countryside the *limitaneus* was a common figure, while roads, bridgeheads, and hundreds of miles of frontier received a guard of *burgarii*. In the relatively untroubled and lightly held provinces of Egypt there were, by about A.D. 300, at least sixty different emplacements of troops. Here it must have been hard to get away from army centers, let alone avoid the soldier as trader, as tax collector, judge, policeman, moneylender, farmer, and the soldier forbidden by the Codes simply to "wander."

His influence made its most obvious mark on civilian architecture. Towers, guarded gates, crenelations, moats and so forth, on city walls or on private houses, may be left aside, since they were borrowed only for their usefulness. It is, however, as clear as it is surprising, that early

Christian basilicas draw inspiration from camp headquarters buildings. Town plans, too, resembled camps, and within towns, the "Roman-British" forum followed military models. An explanation for such copying is easy to find. Army architects were in constant use throughout the empire, and the emperor who kept them busiest, Hadrian, "brigaded in cohorts, like legionary soldiers, his carpenters, surveyors, architects, and every type of expert in building walls or in decorating" (Aurel. Vict. *Epit.* 14.5).

This quotation hints at the prestige and convenience of military organization, which, by these qualities, put its stamp on other groups quite unconnected with the army. The most striking examples must be looked for in the civil office staffs of the central government, where the lowliest scribbler wore a military belt, was called *miles*, and, after the completion of his *militia*, *veteranus*; where his superiors were *commentarienses*, *cornicularii*, and the like — all army ranks — and carried the centurion's swagger stick. But the same sort of imitation can be found also in other branches of government — in the *optiones* and *centuriones* commanding the emperor's freedmen; or even among private guilds. Here officers went by the titles of *principales*, *centuriones*, *optiones*; ranks were *centuriae* and *numeri caligatorum*; and members were conducted on "maneuvers." There are religious parallels. Within the body of Mithra's worshippers, "The neophyte, on entering, was bound by an oath (*sacramentum*) like that administered to army recruits, and no doubt also he was branded indelibly, with a hot iron. In the mystical hierarchy, the third grade was 'private' (*miles*): thereafter the initiate formed part of the holy army of the invincible god." Similar military terminology spread to other pagan worships — of Bacchus, Venus, and Isis; above all, it is found in Christian writers, for whom Christ is *imperator*, bishops *duces*, Christians an *exercitus* or "the legion" of *milites*, the laity *gregarii numeri*, neophytes *tirones*, churches *castra*, and so forth. Outside of any such religious context, metaphors drawn from army procedures perhaps enjoyed a special popularity. Libanius speaks of "the office-holder, who has been posted, as it were, for the defense of the laws, to wage war against their every active enemy"; "of an unusually ambitious person, that he was deserting his *taxis*"; and, in this writer at least, other metaphors of war are especially common.

Soldiers have always had words to lend, technical or slang. Some now current in English, from the Air Force, include "zeroed in" (accurately aimed), "bombed" (drunk), and "tail-spin" (panic); but all languages are full of such borrowings. With Latin and Greek, the problem is more complicated. For one thing, there is the role of the army in teaching Latin to barbarians and Greeks. In areas little Romanized, inscriptions become more often Latin, and better and better Latin, as one approaches a legionary camp, from which radiated the chief forces of Romanization. A very large number of words, with only minor changes, were taken over into Greek, and of these, so far as can be seen from papyri, the greatest number before Diocletian were military: *tribounos*, for example, but scores could be listed. Legions in the East, however, because of more local recruiting, contained men whose first language was Greek, and who knew the language of command not at all, or only in the sketchiest fashion. The transference of the world's capital to Constantinople, the gathering flood of constitutions, orders, quadruplicates, and appeals, and the intention of Constantine and of his successors that all this governing should be carried on in Latin, meant for that language a wider spread. Not only did the terms of the bureaucracy spread, but Constantine specifically prescribed Latin for his armies, and in Egypt it remained in official use for army commanders even to the end of the fifth century. Thus army Latin in the East received a second chance to insinuate itself into Greek.

Among words borrowed by Greek and Roman soldiers occur (besides dozens of good Latin ones) some quite foreign examples: *gaesum* (a kind of spear), *sagos* (a Gallic cloak), *droungos* (a tactical formation), *bandon* (a *vexillum*) — these all Celtic — and others also. Most of these were adopted also by Latin, and rapidly naturalized. *Drungus (hoc est globos, hostium*; Veget. 3.16) is used without any special explanation, in SHA *Probus* 19.2; so Gothic *carrago*, perhaps a kind of cart, in Ammianus 31.7.7 and in SHA *Aurelian* 11.6. This is the process of barbarization in which the army played such a key part. There are also, however, words of a better origin, but distorted by soldiers into some new use: slang or metaphor. A "butterfly" (*papilio*) is a tent, found not only in a handbook of camp planning but also in Tertullian, the Vulgate, and often in the Scriptores Historiae Augustae. *Conterraneus*, "countryman," *hoc castrense verbum* (Plin. *N. H.* praef. 1 D), passed into wider use in vulgar Latin (*TLL* s.v.), and *focaria* ("army wife") appears without comment in the Digest, in inscriptions, and in a legal document of Severan times. Army corruptions like the invented verg *aquor*, "to water" (active, as of horses) or "to go in search of water," are acceptable even to Vergil: *tutis sub moenibus urbis aquantur*.

Literary purists generally looked down their noses at this military influence as so much barbarism. No doubt the kind of Latin spoken in the army was not elegant. Some soldiers — there is no saying how many — could not even write. Against these we may set the poets in uniform: the camp organist at Aquincum writing his wife's epitaph in verse (*CIL* 3.10501), a centurion of Severan times describing how the camp baths at Bu Ngem came to be built, "to refresh the body with swimming," and a cavalryman in Egypt using poetry to adorn the fact that he had completed a five-month term of armed duty (he misspells "month" *meses*). "In the collection of metrical inscriptions, the epitaphs of soldiers form a large and interesting group." There is, too, the third-century centurion who appears on his sarcophagus reading, facing Polyhymnia; around, other men with books; to the rear, *eight* Muses, including one for the theater; and the whole "glorified an 'intellectual household,' given to study in the company of its masters and under the eye of the Muses." Finally, we may add the soldiers of higher rank, though few, who even in the late Empire took an interest in history and philosophy.

Some indirect idea of the level of literacy in the army can be formed from the orations of Hadrian to several African units. He apparently expected to be understood, if not fully appreciated, even in the use of scattered archaisms, rare words, and preciosities, and in a generally careful style. Yet the *allocutio* was a special occasion, and called for an increasingly self-conscious dignity, in speech and setting. It gathered round it connotations of "The Monarch close to His Loyal Troops." Shown in relief on Trajan's and the Antonine columns and on the arches of Septimius Severus and Constantine, it assumed a greater frontality and formality, "definitive and entirely characteristic for late antique art." It inspired the building of special courts, platforms, and halls, in the very middle of camps, and from these seem to have developed significant features — the triapsidal throne room, the Place of Appearance approached through a sort of open-air basilica — essential to Byzantine court ceremonies. But the influence of a military occasion and of military architecture on court ceremonial goes far beyond the *allocutio*.

The emperor's palace in Rome was, from 193, defended by

"latticed gates and strong doors" (Dio 74.16.4). "And when [the senators] met [Septimius Severus] at Interamna, they were searched for concealed weapons and only then suffered to greet him as he stood armed in the midst of armed men" (SHA *Sept. Severus* 6.2). His first appearance was typical of the man and of the era to come. Yet he did no more than advance further the transformation of the *princeps* into a pure *imperator*, and of palace into camp (*castra*). Everything to do with the emperor — furniture, pages, treasury, everything — was already called *castrensis*, before Septimius Severus ever entered the scene. By Gallienus's time, the emperor's courtiers bore the name *comitatus*, more strikingly in Greek, *stratopedon*. On coins, the common symbol of a towered gate is perhaps to be intepreted, first, as a *castrum*, and the *castrum* then as "an image of the *Sacrum palatium*, from which emanated the universal authority, wisdom, and military virtue of a divine ruler." These visible proofs of change in the emperor's residence and retinue are of course notorious, and their significance cannot be overemphasized. They represent, in a word, militarization. They belong with the emperor clothed in a general's uniform — even that sedentary septuagenarian, Antoninus Pius — or assuming, as his only concession to peace, the mufti of a Roman soldier, the tunic called a dalmatic, which Commodus (who never in his reign left Italy) wore for a reception of the senate, before going on to the theater. More startling are the garments typical of mere privates, adopted by emperors who wished to declare their yet closer identification with their troops: the "G.I." hood (*caracallus*) which gave a name to the second Severan, or the *bracae* (breeches) of Celtic auxiliaries, worn by Julian at his coronation. But then, Julian's reign initiated the crown-ceremony of the torque and "Schilderhebung," the raising of the emperor on a shield. Since his troops had chosen him, it was only right to incorporate their role formally into the coronation ceremonies; since he was to assume a position of emperor-soldier, he was only beginning as he must go on.

Uniforms are loved by the military because they give at once distinction between ranks and identity within a rank. In Roman civil society, a particular dress had long been usual and sometimes obligatory for public slaves. It was marked by a transverse band, the *limus*; its wearers were called *limocincti*. The toga was forbidden them. Higher up, senators and equestrians had their separate stripes; and all wore a toga as opposed to the standard cloak, *caligae*, and other garments of wartime; but these distinctions, though very important, were not at first elaborated. Only in the third-century army did regular soldiers assume the red leather *cingulum* and a whitish chlamys with a purple inset, and whitish trousers, and a tunic with colored insignia on it. In these articles and in other details of dress and armor, differences in color, weight, and ornament showed the various ranks, though whether these differences were fixed and symbolic, or only matters of relative richness, is obscure. A system similar, perhaps less refined, worked well enough in the Middle Ages. It was Severus Alexander's intention "to assign a peculiar type of clothing to each imperial staff, not only to various ranks — in order that they might be distinguished by their garments — but also to the slaves as a class — that they might be easily recognized" (SHA *Severus Alex*. 27.1–2). Though the scheme was scotched for this reign by Paul and Ulpian, it came to life again in the fourth century as an indirect result of the militarization of the civil service. Clerks and secretaries retained the uniform of the soldiers from whom they were descended. *Cingulum* occurs often as meaning "office," and *discingere* "to discharge from office." Ranks were marked in dress. Yet the most fundamental distinction lay naturally between civilian (holding no office at all) and "military," in the late imperial sense (in the armed or civil service). Those who were not *milites* were strictly ordered to hold to civilian clothing. Roman senators objected. A compromise specified togas only for senate meetings. "No senator shall vindicate for himself the *habitus militaris*, but, leaving aside the terror of the general's chlamys, put on the garments of peace. . . . Staff members shall also wear civilian cloaks (*paenula*), but shall hold their inner garments closely bound by means of their *cingulum* in such a way, however, that they shall cover their breasts with variegated mantles, and thus by such acknowledgment they shall bear witness to the necessities of their ignoble status." The text shows conveniently the two most important things about uniforms: that they somehow differed by rank, and that the prestige of wearing them was tremendous. They were usurped by private citizens for improper purposes; they permeated government; they reached even to the eunuchs of the court, who "gave themselves airs on the strength of their liveries."

This visible marking of distinctions meant (since the great men of the empire were so commonly active or honorary members of the government) that the aristocracy as such wore uniform. Purple, gold thread, precious stones, and silk were generally reserved for the emperor and his family; the *cingulum*, chlamys, and a certain specified luxury of dress, for his servants, in what has been called "a hierarchy through clothing." One could tell such men in the streets. One addressed them, according to the degree of their importance, by such almost technical terms as *spectabilis*, *laudabilis*, *egregius*, *venerabilis*, *perfectissimus*, *sacer*, and *eminentissimus*. In formal assemblies, they were marshaled by costume, title, and "conformably with military usage, a strict order of advancement by seniority of service." The passion for rank produced, first, a profusion of official positions, each with its appropriate forms of address; then, a division of each, into several classes; finally, a subdivision according to the mode and very hour of promotion.

From their eminence, these government dignitaries surveyed an entire population assigned to ranks. Several social levels were recognized, and were entitled to different treatment before the law — slaves and *coloni*, *humiliores* and *honestiores*. Every individual was fixed in his spot, except the "sturdy beggar," whom it was a duty to seize and immobilize in the first vacant role that came handy. Armorers, bakers, clerks, doctors, farmers, all had their place, and transmitted it to their heirs, and could not leave for another town, nor take up another occupation, nor even marry freely beyond their appointed boundaries. In practice, considerable movement remained. In theory, the whole population of the empire, as if in an indefinite state of emergency, stood sentinel over some post or function.

This system prevailed certainly by the death of Constantine, however much elaboration it underwent later. Its beginnings have of course been eagerly sought, but in the search, historians are hampered by the dark period before the 290s. It would be safe to say only that development toward universal conscription of Roman society, as it appears in the light of the Codes, was enormously accelerated in the last thirty or forty years of the third century.

What sort of men could it be who would so completely and minutely destroy the freedom of a society? To the conditions of the times, why did that one response seem the natural one, which was actually offered by the later Empire?

Emperors who were the most important historically in the last generation or two of the third century include Aureolus, Gallienus, Claudius, Aurelian, Probus, Carus, Diocletian, Maximian, and Constantius Chlorus. All "of humble birth, and most often uncultivated, the only avenue of success was for them a military one." Their right-hand men, the praetorian prefects, seem to have been without exception men of strictly military background; within their inner council was "a military committee" of *militares*; and they used, as their confidential agents, military police and tribunes, to bind the empire together in a web of espionage. There can be no doubt whatever that the forming influence in the crisis of the later Empire was the military mind.

Over the last four or five centuries, the characteristic behavior of soldiers has suggested very powerfully the effect of army life on ways of thinking. Where one can study it in reasonable detail, there does indeed seem to be a "military mind." It exhibits two loves: of precedent and of rank. As to the first, military training is based on examples from times long past, in procedures long frozen to a set form. It is "by the book," and the principle of seniority tends to place instruction and command in the hands of old men. The army is subject to "outbursts of organizational rigidity which remain baffling to the civilian outsider. Anachronistic survivals are practiced alongside highly effective procedures of military management. Much of the ritualism of the military profession — the constant, minute, and repeated inspection of person and property — are devices which are to be found in any occupation where the risks of personal danger are great. Ritualism is in part a defense against anxiety, but it is also a device for wedding tradition to innovation." Subservience to the past, a dislike of risky change, and a fundamental conservatism mark the soldier.

One can see, too, especially in Prussia, a "hideous spirit of fearful obedience to authority"; but generally, a manner of thinking of people and powers as a ladder. Orders come down from above, obedience is directed upward. There is a fixed place for everyone, and a hierarchy for everything. As late as the eighteenth century, cavalry outranked artillery, and won the honor of the right flank; in the officers' parties of a twentieth-century garrison post, the colonel's lady poured the coffee, because "coffee outranks tea." There is a tendency to see things vertically.

These two loves moved the Roman army. Surely nothing need be said of the love of rank. But to do things by the book was clearly the common practice, too. Military architects give an illustration. Best known are their straight, even roads, and their towers along fortified stretches of the frontiers, at precisely fixed intervals. Some other examples have been mentioned earlier: the standardized house plans in *canabae*; the standardized town walls, in Gaul and Spain; the standardized entranceways, turrets, and the like, in Wales, and (really remarkable) in Africa the line of fortresses, some of which were rebuilt to conform better to a single model. Camp design achieved a specially elaborate, almost ritualistic, uniformity from its general layout down to the smallest detail, attested in scores of excavations; but there are the minute instructions of Vegetius (1.21 ff.): the ditch, for instance, is to be dug, "so that it is twelve feet wide and nine feet 'under the line,' as they say (that is, perpendicular)"; and when it is finished, "it is inspected and measured by the centurions, who punish such as have been indolent or negligent." Reminiscent of this are the words of command, unchanged over five or six centuries . . . , and the style of military inscriptions exhibiting "a remarkable consistency throughout the first and second centuries, and in the early third century A.D."; at Corbridge, arms manufacture was carried on in the same way. "The great variety of the weapons, of which each class is clearly standardized within itself, is almost unexpected. It would seem that arrows and darts were classified not only by size and weight, but differently barbed according to the work they had to do." Parade helmets had a specified weight of precious metal on them. And if we turn to an area of activity far removed from these various examples, we find even army worships, the calendar of sacrifices, and the roll of admissable gods regulated on one plan throughout the empire, regardless of local preferences. Soldiers in Dura, in the third century, still celebrated, doubtless with no understanding of what they were doing, the old Italian peasant festivals.

A minute obedience to authorized precedent, and a tendency to reduce men to fixed positions, arranged in a careful hierarchy — these are characteristic of the military mind, Roman or later. Moreover, in the hundred years stretching from roughly A.D. 250 on, it was soldiers who were in a position to form opinion and make changes. It should follow that the characteristic developments of the decline reflect the thought of the Roman army.

This possibility has never been given a fair chance, so to speak. It has been thrust aside by a more popular alternative: the derivation of social, economic, administrative, and constitutional features of the late Empire from the East. To explain such things as state monopolies, hierarchization of society, and even innovations in camp architecture, scholars have ransacked Egypt, Syria, and Persia, from Hellenistic to Sassanian times. At their worst, they have attributed to the men in power, in Rome and Constantinople, such knowledge as one might expect only in some curator of Near Eastern antiquities; but "barrack generals," under pressure of emergency, meeting in great haste the most complex difficulties, surely did not look for help in the vestigial practices of their eastern provinces. They themselves and the agents they trusted came from the North. They knew little that they had not learned in the camp. They had time to act only instinctively, and their instincts were military.

The present study suggests only a tool of explanation. Others may perhaps test its usefulness. The later Empire was to some extent militarized. The emperor, for example, drew closer to his troops, and the balance of power and prestige inclined, under Septimius Severus, towards army officers. So much is generally admitted. The greater part of army influence, in various fields, which has been traced in previous chapters [of *Soldier and Civilian*], has been detected, if not emphasized, by other scholars. What might be tried, however, is a somewhat more confident use of such material to explain wider developments. Take, for illustration, Diocletian's reign, crucial in itself, and occurring in the very middle of our period. Was it, in general character, really a complex of violent changes, or was it as essentially conservative as we might expect from a man of strictly military background? Was Diocletian's reform of taxes modeled on Egyptian and Syrian experiments, or was it, in its basic term *iugatio*, and in its rigid simplicity, just such as a conservative commissary officer might choose? Was his treatment of the civil service radical, or only (for a soldier) logical? Was the further freezing of his subjects in different grades and functions the work of Oriental despotism, or of an impatient commander ignorant of civilian liberties? And did the design of his palace come from the East, or was it not rather created by army architects, using the traditions of Roman castrametation? To these questions, the second answers seem more persuasive.

East, West, and the Barbarians

A. H. M. Jones

The Pressure of the Barbarians

Why Did the Western Empire Fall?

The causes of the fall of the western empire in the fifth century have been endlessly debated since Augustine's day, but those who have debated the question have all been westerners, and have tended to forget that the eastern empire did not fall until many centuries later. Many of the causes alleged for the fall of the west were common to the east, and therefore cannot be complete and self-sufficient causes. If, as the pagans said in 410, it was the gods, incensed by the apostasy of the empire, who struck it down, why did they not strike down the equally Christian eastern parts? If, as Salvian argues, it was God who sent the barbarians to chastise the sinful Romans, why did He not send barbarians to chastise the equally sinful Constantinopolitans? If Christianity, as Gibbon thought, sapped the empire's morale and weakened it by internal schisms, why did not the more Christian east, with its much more virulent theological disputes, fall first?

We must look then for points in which the two halves of the empire differed. In the first place the western provinces were much more exposed to barbarian attack. The western emperor had to guard the long fronts of the Rhine and the upper Danube, the eastern emperor only the lower Danube. For on the eastern front his neighbor was the Persian empire, a civilized power which was not on the whole aggressive and kept its treaties. If a Persian war broke out, it was a more serious affair than a barbarian invasion, but wars were rare until the sixth century, and they then tested the Roman empire very severely. Moreover, if the western emperor failed to hold any part of the Rhine and Danube fronts, he had no second line of defense; the invaders could penetrate straight into Italy and Gaul, and even into Spain. The eastern emperor, if he failed, as he often did, to hold the lower Danube, only lost control temporarily of the European dioceses; for no enemy could force the Bosphorus and the Hellespont, guarded by Constantinople itself. Asia Minor, Syria and Egypt thus remained sealed off from invasion.

The barbarian invaders soon grasped the strategical position and, even if they first crossed the lower Danube and ravaged Thrace and Illyricum, soon tired of these exhausted lands and, unable to penetrate into the rich lands of Asia Minor, trekked westwards to Italy. This path was successively followed by the Visigoths under Alaric and the Ostrogoths under Theoderic.

In the second place the eastern parts were probably more populous, more intensively cultivated and richer than the western. This is hard to prove and difficult to believe nowadays, when the Balkans, Asia Minor and Syria are poor and thinly peopled, and only Egypt is rich and populous, whereas in the west Italy, France, Britain and the Low Countries are wealthy and densely populated, and only north Africa is poor. But many lines of argument suggest that the reverse was true in Roman times. The population of Egypt was about 8 million, that of Gaul (which included besides modern France the Low Countries and Germany west of the Rhine) can be estimated at about 2½ million. The diocese of Egypt yielded perhaps three times as much revenue as that of Africa. Archaeological evidence proves that many areas now desert or waste in Syria and Asia Minor were inhabited and cultivated in late Roman times, and suggest that much of the most fertile soil in northern Gaul and Britain was still uncleared forest. It is moreover possible to estimate the wealth of different areas in the Roman empire from the number and scale of the public buildings of the cities, since the rich put much of their surplus wealth into such buildings. On this test the Mediterranean lands, eastern and southern Spain, southern Gaul, Italy, Africa, the southern Balkans, Asia Minor, Syria and Egypt were all wealthy, and Asia Minor and Syria the wealthiest of all, whereas Britain, northern Gaul and the Danubian lands were miserably poor. This analysis is borne out by literary testimonies. In the west Sardinia, Sicily and above all Africa, were regarded as the richest provinces, the granaries of the empire, and Aquitania as more fertile than northern Gaul. This implies that the potential fertility of the northern plains had not yet been exploited to the full.

In some other ways the east was superior to the west. It enjoyed much greater political stability and less of its resources were wasted in civil wars. From the accession of Diocletian in 284 to the death of Maurice in 602 there were only five attempted usurpations, those of Domitius Domitianus under Diocletian, of Procopius under Valens, of Basiliscus, Marcian and Leontius under Zeno, and all were quickly subdued without many casualties. In the west there were rebellions or usurpations by Carausius, Maxentius, Alexander, Magnentius, Firmus, Magnus Maximus, Gildo, Constantine, Jovinus and John, most of which involved heavy fighting, and after the death of Valentinian III a succession of ephemeral emperors.

The social and economic structure of the east was healthier than that of the west. In the east more of the land was owned by peasant proprietors, who paid taxes only, and thus a larger proportion of the total yield of agriculture went to the peasantry. In the west a much higher proportion of the land was owned by great landlords, whose tenants had to pay rents in excess of their taxes, and the general condition of the peasantry was therefore poorer. This is reflected in the recurrent revolts of the Bacaudae in Gaul and Spain, which at times contained troops urgently needed elsewhere.

Another result of this difference in social structure was that the landed aristocracy in the west obtained a stranglehold on the administration, with two deleterious results. They were inefficient administrators, and allowed the bureaucracy to add a very appreciable sum to the burden of taxation by their exorbitant fees. They were overindulgent to their own class, and slack in curbing grants of immunity and reductions and remissions of taxes. In the east the administrative machine remained in the hands of men of middle-class origin, who owed their advancement to the imperial government; they kept the expenses of tax collection down to a very reasonable figure, and periodically cancelled reductions of tax granted to landowners. A higher proportion of the total yield of agriculture thus reached the imperial treasury, and less was absorbed by the bureaucracy and by landlords.

Another question may be asked. When the western empire had stood firm for two and a half centuries from the reign of Augustus, and had surmounted the crisis of the mid-third century, and, reorganized by Diocletian, had maintained itself intact for another three generations, why did it so rapidly collapse in the fifth century? Was the collapse primarily due to increased outside pressure or to internal decay or to a mixture of both?

One can only approximately gauge the external pressure on the empire. If one compares two historians who wrote on a similar scale of the first and of the fourth centuries A.D., Tacitus and Ammianus, one gains the impression that in the former period there was no heavy pressure on the frontiers, but in general peace, with only occasional border wars, whereas in the latter the emperors were constantly engaged in checking a breakthrough here and another breakthrough there. The first serious attack on the Roman frontier was under Marcus Aurelius, and in the mid-third century the migrations of the Goths and other East German tribes set up a general movement along the Danube, while the West German tribes grouped in the Frankish and Alamannic federation became more aggressive. The emperors of the late third century managed to restore the line, but it was henceforth held with far more effort than before. In the third quarter of the fourth century the westward movement of the Huns set all the German tribes in motion, and their pressure on the empire was redoubled. The tremendous losses incurred by the western Roman army during this period, amounting it would seem to two-thirds of its effectives, are striking evidence of the severity of the barbarian attacks.

One cause of weakness to the western parts was their administrative separation from the east. Formerly the emperors had been able to draw freely on the wealth of the east to finance the defense of the west. From the time of Diocletian the relatively poor western parts had to make do on their own resources with only occasional aid from the east.

To meet the increased barbarian pressure both halves of the empire enormously increased their armed forces, probably doubling their numbers. How far the high standard of military efficiency established in the principate was kept up, it is difficult to say, but it is unlikely that there was any significant decline. As any reader of Tacitus knows, the army of the early principate was not perfect. In peaceful times discipline became very slack, and the men spent their days on their private avocations and rarely attended a parade. Troops could get out of hand and plunder the provinces they were supposed to protect, and could panic in the face of the enemy. The officers were not professional soldiers and were often incompetent. These and other weaknesses appear in the later Roman empire, but the officers were on the whole of better quality, being experienced professionals. Small bodies of Roman troops still could and did defeat very much larger barbarian hordes in the fourth, fifth and sixth centuries.

The heavy economic burden imposed by the increased size of the army overstrained the resources of the empire and produced a number of weaknesses. It may seem an exaggeration to say that the resources of so large an area as the Roman Empire could be overstrained by feeding, clothing and arming an extra 300,000 men, but it must be remembered that the empire was technologically even more backward than Europe of the Middle Ages. With primitive methods of agriculture, industrial production and transport it took very many more man-hours than today to produce the food for rations, to weave the fabrics for uniforms, to hammer out the arms and armor and to transport all this material by barge and wagon to the frontiers. Taxation had to be enormously increased, and to assess and collect the increased taxes, the civil service had to be expanded, thus increasing the taxation load again.

The heavy burden of taxation was probably the root cause of the economic decline of the empire. Marginal lands, which could not yield a profit to the landlord over and above the taxes, ceased to be cultivated. The population seems also to have shrunk. This is a highly disputable point, but there are distinct signs of a chronic shortage of agricultural manpower, notably the reluctance of landlords to surrender their tenants as recruits, the legislation tying tenants to their farms, the constant attempts of landlords to filch tenants from their neighbors, and the large-scale settlement of barbarians on the land. The shortage was not due to a flight from the land to the towns — the movement was rather in the opposite direction. It was exacerbated by the demands of conscription, but it is difficult to resist the suggestion that the peasant population failed to maintain its numbers. The decline in the cultivated area, though not primarily due to manpower shortage, implies that the rural population did decline. The reason for this was that the peasantry, after paying their taxes, and the tenants their rent, did not retain enough food to rear large families, and many died of malnutrition or of actual starvation in bad seasons or after enemy devastations.

Ideally speaking the empire could of course have reduced the economic burden by rigid efficiency and drastic pruning of superfluities. It maintained large numbers of idle or nominal soldiers and sinecurist civil servants. According to old custom it fed 120,000 citizens of Rome, and added to these 80,000 citizens of Constantinople. These were a direct burden on the treasury. It also tolerated, and indeed encouraged, the growth of other classes of idle mouths, notably the clergy. Paganism had cost very little, its priests, except in Egypt, receiving no remuneration except portions of sacrifices. The churches, with their many thousands of clergy, maintained from agricultural rents and first fruits, constituted a new and substantial burden on the economy. The emperors moreover did nothing to curb the growth of the official aristocracy in numbers and wealth, and thus tolerated and encouraged the increase of another unproductive class.

The basic cause of the economic decline of the empire was in fact the increasing number of (economically speaking) idle mouths — senators with their vast households, decurions, civil servants, lawyers, soldiers, clergy, citizens of the capitals — as compared with the number of producers. The resultant burden of taxation and rents proved too much for the peasantry, who slowly dwindled in numbers.

It has been argued that the empire was weakened by the decay of its trade and industry. It is in fact very doubtful if trade and industry did decay: the production and distribution of high-grade and luxury goods for the rich certainly continued to flourish down to the sixth century, and the bulk of industrial and commercial activity had probably always been devoted to such goods. In any event industry and trade had at all times made so small a contribution to the national income that their decay, if it did occur, was economically unimportant.

This economic pressure was, it must be remembered, as severe in the eastern as in the western parts. The east maintained as large an army and a civil service, and had an even larger and richer body of clergy, if a less wealthy aristocracy, than the west. Its rate of taxation was very high, its marginal lands fell out of cultivation, and its population probably sank. But it had greater reserves of agricultural wealth and manpower on which to draw.

No one who reads the scanty records of the collapse of the western empire can fail to be struck by the apathy of the Roman population from the highest to the lowest. The only instance of concerted self-help by the provincials is the action of the cities of Britain and Armorica in 408, when, failing to receive aid from the usurper Constantine, they organized their own defense against the barbarians, with the subsequent approval of Honorius. In 471-75 Sidonius Apollinaris, the bishop of their city, inspired the Arverni to defend themselves against the

Visigoths. In 532 Pudentius raised his province of Tripolitania against the Vandals and, with the aid of a small imperial force, ejected them. In 546 Tullianus, a landlord of Lucania and Bruttium, organized a large body of peasants, which assisted the imperial forces against Totila. These are the only resistance movements of which we know. Elsewhere the upper classes either fled — there is ample evidence for Spain in 409, when the barbarians first broke in, and for the African provinces in 437 and 442, when the Vandals invaded them — or stayed put and collaborated with the barbarian kings. Not that they were active traitors, with one or two notorious exceptions, but they passively accepted their lot. They were very pleased in Africa and Italy when Justinian's armies arrived, but they did very little to help them.

The lower classes were just as inert. Townsmen would generally man the walls, but their object was to avoid a sack, and if guaranteed security they would usually surrender. Peasants, like their betters, sometimes fled in panic, but more often accepted their fate passively. They would fight if given a lead, as by Tullianus, but they would fight on either side. Totila subsequently ordered the landlords under his control to recall their peasants from Tullianus's force, and they meekly obeyed. Later Totila raised his own force of Italian peasants and they fought their fellow-citizens under Tullianus in bloody battles. Among the lower classes again there is very little evidence of active cooperation with the barbarians. In fact only one case is known; in 376 some Thracian miners joined the Goths and guided them to rich villas where stores of food were available. Having recently been recalled to their work from agriculture, they may have had a special grievance. It is alleged by Salvian that some peasants in Gaul fled to the barbarians to escape the oppression of landords and tax collectors; this is no doubt true, but Salvian is a biased witness and perhaps exaggerates.

This apathy was not peculiar to the western parts; instances of self-help are as rare in the east. Nor was it, so far as we know, anything new. There had been less occasion for civilian resistance to the enemy under the principate, when the armies on the whole held the invaders at the frontier, but no civilian action is recorded when a breakthrough did occur. For many centuries the provincials had been used to being protected by a professional army, and they had indeed, ever since the reign of Augustus, been prohibited by the *lex lulia de vi* from bearing arms; this law was in force and more or less observed in the fifth century, and Justinian stiffened it by making the manufacture of arms a strict government monopoly. It was only on the rarest occasions that the government appealed to the civil population (including slaves) to take up arms to defend the empire; in 406 when Radagaesus with his horde had broken into Italy, the government appealed for volunteers "for love of peace and country," and in 440, when Gaiseric was threatening to invade Italy, it authorized the provincials to arm themselves to resist Vandal landing parties. It is not known whether either appeal was fruitful; in earlier crises Augustus and Marcus Aurelius had been obliged to apply conscription in Italy.

The general attitude of the provincials to the empire was, and always had been, passive. This is well illustrated under the principate by such panegyrics on the Roman empire as that of Aelius Aristides, and by the provincial cult of Rome and Augustus. Provincials were profoundly grateful to the empire for protecting them from the barbarians and maintaining internal security, and thus enabling them to enjoy and develop the amenities of civilized life in peace. But they felt no active loyalty, no obligation to help the emperor in his task. He was a god, whom they delighted to worship, but who needed no aid from his mortal subjects.

It has been argued that the regimentation of the population into hereditary castes led to interia and discontent. It is true that many members of the classes affected tried to evade their hereditary obligations, but this does not prove that all were discontented. In any society, however free, most people are content to carry on in their parents' vocation, and it is only an enterprising few who strike out a new line and rise in the social scale. So far as we can tell the enterprising few in the later Roman empire normally succeeded in flouting or evading the law, which was very inefficiently enforced. The extent and the rigidity of the caste system have in any case been exaggerated, and it was, it may be noted, common to both east and west.

There was undoubtedly a decline in public spirit in the later Roman empire, both in the east and in the west. Under the principate there had existed a strong sense of civic patriotism among the gentry, and they had given freely of their time and money not only to improve the amenities of their cities, but to perform many administrative tasks, such as collecting the taxes and levying recruits, delegated to the cities by the imperial government. From the third century onwards this civic patriotism faded, and the imperial government had to rely more and more on its own administrators and civil servants. Under the principate the service of the state had been regarded as a high duty, incumbent on the imperial aristocracy, and on the whole, the government service being small and select, high standards were maintained. Under the later empire the old pagan idea of public service waned and the church taught good Christians to regard the imperial service as dirty work, if not sinful, while the ranks of the administration were greatly expanded and its quality inevitably diluted. Hence the growth of corruption and extortion, leading to popular discontent and waste of the limited resources of the empire. Over a wider field the teaching of the church that salvation was only to be found in the world to come and that the things of this world did not matter may have encouraged apathy and defeatism.

It must however be emphasized that the eastern empire shared to the full these various weaknesses, economic, social and moral, and that it nevertheless survived for centuries as a great power. It was the increasing pressure of the barbarians, concentrated on the weaker western half of the empire, that caused the collapse.

Ammianus Marcellinus

The Huns

Ammianus Marcellinus, c. A.D. 330–395, was a Greek from Antioch who served in the Roman army. He wrote a history of Rome, continuing the work of Tacitus, from 96 to 378. In the following selection he speaks of the Huns, one of the barbarian tribes that pressed on the Roman Empire and ultimately brought it down.

The people called Huns, barely mentioned in ancient records, live beyond the sea of Azof, on the border of the Frozen Ocean, and are

From Ammianus Marcellinus, *Res Gestae*, trans. C. D. Yonge (1862), 3.1, 2–4, 13.

a race savage beyond all parallel. At the very moment of birth the cheeks of their infant children are deeply marked by an iron, in order that the hair, instead of growing at the proper season on their faces, may be hindered by the scars; accordingly the Huns grow up without beards, and without any beauty. They all have closely knit and strong limbs and plump necks; they are of great size, and low legged, so that you might fancy them two-legged beasts or the stout figures which are hewn out in a rude manner with an ax on the posts at the end of bridges.

They are certainly in the shape of men, however uncouth, and are so hardy that they neither require fire nor well-flavored food, but live on the roots of such herbs as they get in the fields, or on the half-raw flesh of any animal, which they merely warm rapidly by placing it between their own thighs and the backs of their horses.

They never shelter themselves under roofed houses, but avoid them, as people ordinarily avoid sepulchers as things not fit for common use. Nor is there even to be found among them a cabin thatched with reeds; but they wander about, roaming over the mountains and the woods, and accustom themselves to bear frost and hunger and thirst from their very cradles. . . .

There is not a person in the whole nation who cannot remain on his horse day and night. On horseback they buy and sell, they take their meat and drink, and there they recline on the narrow neck of their steed, and yield to sleep so deep as to indulge in every variety of dream.

And when any deliberation is to take place on any weighty matter, they all hold their common council on horseback. They are not under kingly authority, but are contented with the irregular government of their chiefs, and under their lead they force their way through all obstacles. . . .

None of them plow, or even touch a plow handle, for they have no settled abode, but are homeless and lawless, perpetually wandering with their wagons, which they make their homes; in fact, they seem to be people always in flight. . . .

This active and indomitable race, being excited by an unrestrained desire of plundering the possessions of others, went on ravaging and slaughtering all the nations in their neighborhood till they reached the Alani. . . .

[After having harassed the territory of the Alani and having slain many of them and acquired much plunder, the Huns made a treaty of friendship and alliance with those who survived. The allies then attacked the German people to the west.] In the meantime a report spread far and wide through the nations of the Goths, that a race of men, hitherto unknown, had suddenly descended like a whirlwind from the lofty mountains, as if they had risen from some secret recess of the earth, and were ravaging and destroying everything which came in their way.

And then the greater part of the population resolved to flee and seek a home remote from all knowledge of the new barbarians; and after long deliberation as to where to fix their abode, they resolved that a retreat into Thrace was the most suitable for these two reasons; first of all, because it is a district most fertile in grass; and secondly, because, owing to the great breadth of the Danube, it is wholly separated from the districts exposed to the impending attacks of the invaders.

Accordingly, under the command of their leader Alavivus, they occupied the banks of the Danube, and sent ambassadors to the emperor Valens, humbly entreating to be received by him as his subjects. They promised to live quietly, and to furnish a body of auxiliary troops if necessary.

While these events were taking place abroad, the terrifying rumor reached us that the tribes of the north were planning new and unprecedented attacks upon us; and that over the whole region which extends from the country of the Marcomanni and Quadi to Pontus, hosts of barbarians composed of various nations, which had suddenly been driven by force from their own countries, were now, with all their families, wandering about in different directions on the banks of the river Danube.

At first this intelligence was lightly treated by our people, because they were not in the habit of hearing of any wars in those remote districts till they were terminated either by victory or by treaty.

But presently the belief in these occurrences grew stronger and was confirmed by the arrival of ambassadors, who, with prayers and earnest entreaties, begged that their people, thus driven from their homes and now encamped on the other side of the river, might be kindly received by us.

The affair now seemed a cause of joy rather than of fear, according to the skillful flatterers who were always extolling and exaggerating the good fortune of the emperor. They congratulated him that an embassy had come from the farthest corners of the earth, unexpectedly offering him a large body of recruits; and that, by combining the strength of his own people with these foreign forces, he would have an army absolutely invincible. They observed further that the payment for military reenforcements, which came in every year from the provinces, might now be saved and accumulated in his coffers and form a vast treasure of gold.

Full of this hope, he sent forth several officers to bring this ferocious people and their carts into our territory. And such great pains were taken to gratify this nation which was destined to overthrow the Empire of Rome, that no one was left behind, not even of those who were stricken with mortal disease. Moreover, so soon as they had obtained permission of the emperor to cross the Danube and to cultivate some districts in Thrace, they poured across the stream day and night, without ceasing, embarking in troops on board ships and rafts and on canoes made of the hollow trunks of trees. . . .

In this way, through the turbulent zeal of violent people, the ruin of the Roman Empire was brought about. This, at all events, is neither obscure nor uncertain, that the unhappy officers who were intrusted with the charge of conducting the multitude of the barbarians across the river, though they repeatedly endeavored to calculate their numbers, at last abandoned the attempt as hopeless. The man who would wish to ascertain the number might as well (as the most illustrious of poets say) attempt to count the waves in the African sea, or the grains of sand tossed about by the zephyrs. . . .

N. H. Baynes

The Decline of the Roman Empire in Western Europe: Some Modern Explanations

Norman Hepburn Baynes was born in England in 1877 and educated at Oxford. A specialist in late Roman and Byzantine history, he held the chair of Byzantine History at the University of London. Among his more important writings are *The Historia Augusta: Its Date and Purpose*, and *Byzantium*, edited with H. St.-L. B. Moss. His best known work is the masterly survey, *The Byzantine Empire.*

It is the purpose of this paper to consider a few of the more outstanding contributions towards the solution of this familiar problem propounded since the publication in 1898 of Sir Samuel Dill's book on *Roman Society in the last century of the Western Empire* (2nd ed., 1899). It may well appear somewhat surprising that I should venture to speak on such a topic, since my own work, such as it is, has been concerned rather with the history of the Byzantine Empire. And yet for a student of Byzantine history the problem has a special interest: he is forced to consider that problem not merely as a West European issue, but rather to compare and contrast the historical development in the western and eastern provinces of the Empire. He is compelled to raise the question: Why was it that the Roman Empire failed to survive in Western Europe while it endured for a further millennium in the East? The very fact that he is primarily interested in the history of the Byzantine Empire enables him to approach the Western problem from a different angle and to treat that problem in a wider setting and not in isolation. That

Reprinted from the *Journal of Roman Studies* 33 (1943): 29–35, by permission of the Society for the Promotion of Roman Studies.

is my apologia for what might otherwise appear to be an inexcusable impertinence. In a word I desire to ask what general considerations can be adduced to explain the fact, that in Western Europe there is a cultural break — a caesura — while in the East Roman world the cultural development is continuous, the Hellenistic and Roman traditions being gradually fused to form the civilization of the Byzantine Empire.

Of the recent explanations of the decline of the Roman power in Western Europe we may first take that of Vladimir G. Simkhovitch who in the *Political Science Quarterly* for 1916 published an article under the title "Rome's Fall Reconsidered" in which he attributed the collapse of the Roman power to the exhaustion of the soil of Italy and of the provinces. That article has been reprinted — somewhat incongruously — in the author's book *Towards the Understanding of Jesus*. The evil began under the Republic: in Cato's time agriculture had already declined in the greater part of Italy. When asked what is the most profitable thing in the management of one's estate he replied "Good pasturage." What is the next best? "Fairly good pasturage." What is the third best? "Bad pasturage." And the fourth best? "Arare" — agriculture. Simkhovitch admits that the Romans possessed great agricultural knowledge. "All that is implied by the agricultural revolution," he writes, "the seeding of grasses and legumes, the rotation of crops, yes even green manuring, all that was perfectly known to the Romans. Why was it not practiced for two thousand years or more? I do not know." Columella was already drawing upon a literary tradition in his counsel to farmers: his mistakes prove that he had never witnessed the operations which he describes. To seed alfalfa one cyathus for 50 square feet, which amounts to several bushels per acre, is an impossible proposition. Province after province was turned by Rome into a desert: draining was neglected, and deserted fields became mosquito- and malaria-infested swamps. The "inner decay" of the Roman Empire in all its manifold manifestations was in the last analysis entirely based upon the endless stretches of barren, sterile, and abandoned fields in Italy and the provinces. The evidence adduced by Simkhovitch is drawn for the most part from writers of the Republic or of the period of the early Principate, but from the Christian Empire he quotes Constantine's legislation in favor of the children of the poor who have not the means to provide for their offspring, and also the constitution of

Valentinian, Arcadius and Theodosius giving permission to the squatter to cultivate deserted fields. Against those who would maintain that the flight from the land was caused by oppressive taxation he contends that it was precisely the exhaustion of the soil which rendered the burden of taxation oppressive: it was because so much land was uncultivated that taxation pressed so heavily upon those who still continued the farming of their fields. The limits which confine the productivity of man's labor become for society physical conditions of existence from which it cannot escape. It was these limits set by the exhaustion of the soil which rendered the doom of Rome inevitable.

There is no doubt truth in this picture of the decline of agriculture: for the later Empire it may well be an accurate description of some parts of Italy: in A.D. 395 the abandoned fields of Campania alone amounted to something over 528,000 *jugera*; but in itself it is inadequate as an explanation of the fall of Rome. For in one country at least — Egypt — there can be no question of soil-exhaustion, and it is precisely from Egypt that we have our earliest reports of the flight from the land, of the disappearance of villages through depopulation. Modern studies of economic conditions in Egypt have demonstrated the fatal effects of the methods of administrative exploitation employed by the Roman government in that province. The burden of taxation here certainly came first, and the decay of agriculture was its result and not its cause. Further, the sweeping generalizations of Simkhovitch's paper cannot be sustained: even in the fifth century of our era where a resident proprietor supervised the cultivation of his own estate there can be no question of soil-exhaustion. Read again Ausonius's poem of his expedition in the valley of the Moselle, read the letters of Sidonius Apollinaris: still in the Gaul of the fifth century it is clear that there were smiling fields and well-cultivated farms. The real danger of the *latifundia* lay, I am convinced, in the fact that they were for the most part managed by bailiffs for owners who were absentee landlords, men who drew money from their estates in order to spend it in Rome, Ravenna, or some provincial capital. The primary cause of the agricultural decline is to be found in the abuses of the fiscal system, in the scourge of corporate responsibility for the collection of the taxes which ruined the municipal aristocracy of the city *curiae*, and perhaps above all in the absence of the personal supervision of the proprietor and the unprincipled use of authority by irresponsible bailiffs, controlling the cultivation of the large estates which now absorbed so great a part of the land of the empire. Soil-exhaustion is, in fact, an inadequate explanation of the collapse of the Roman power.

Another theory has been proposed by Professor Ellsworth Huntington — that of climatic change. The great sequoias of California — the big trees of a familiar advertisement — have been growing for some three or even four thousand years. Each year in the trunk of the tree there is clearly marked the circle of the year's growth: when the tree is felled these rings can be traced and according to their width a chronological chart of climatic variation can be established: the years of considerable width of ring recording the effect of favorable climatic conditions, the narrower rings marking the result of less favorable climate. In this way for the area of the sequoias the variations in climate can be traced for at least 3,000 years. On this basis Ellsworth Huntington constructed his theory. In an article published in 1917 in the *Quarterly Journal of Economics* on "Climatic Change and Agricultural Exhaustion as Elements in the Fall of Rome" he suggested that the climate of the Mediterranean world and that of California have always undergone similar modifications: that from the chronological chart of Californian climate one is accordingly entitled to reconstruct the changes in the climate of the Mediterranean area during the course of the history of Rome, and from the record of such changes we may conclude that the fall of Rome was due to a decline in the rainfall from which the Mediterranean world suffered during the fourth, fifth, and sixth centuries of our era. It is easy to object that on Professor Huntington's own showing the latter part of the second century and the first half of the third century marked a climatic improvement: it might be hard to trace any corresponding increase in prosperity in the history of the Empire during this period. But a more serious objection would point to the hazardous character of the fundamental assumption. Records of rainfall in the neighborhood of the great trees have only been kept for about half a century; Professor Huntington prints a table of four year-groups in order to establish the climatic parallelism between California and the Mediterranean area (*Quarterly Journal of Economics* xxxi, 1916–17, 193):

I. Seven years of heaviest rainfall in California
II. Eighteen years with heavy rainfall in California
III. Seventeen years with light rainfall in California
IV. Thirteen years with least rainfall in California

The table presents the following figures:

	San Francisco	*Rome*	*Naples*
I.	8.3 in.	10.7 in.	11.5 in.
II.	4.5 in.	10.6 in.	11.0 in.
III.	3.4 in.	9.8 in.	9.2 in.
IV.	1.9 in.	9.6 in.	8.6 in.

"The columns vary," writes Professor Huntington, "in harmony with the California rainfall." That is true, but the disparity in the amount of the decline in rainfall between California and Rome — in California a fall from 8.3 in. to 1.9 in., in Rome a fall only from 10.7 in. to 9.6 in. — is very striking, and it is not easy to see what conclusions can justifiably be drawn from such figures.

But that is not all: the matter does not remain as it stood in 1917. In 1925 the Carnegie Institute of Washington published further discussion of the Big Tree as a climatic measure, and it now appears uncertain what part is played respectively by temperature and what by rainfall in the yearly growth. Thus a further element of ambiguity is introduced into the problem. Before this Ossa of doubt piled upon a Pelion of uncertainty the confidence of a mere student of history may well quail, and for the present I should hesitate to call in aid Nature's yardstick as a solution of our historical perplexities. The great trees still keep their climatic secret.

From Nature we may turn to the human factor in our search for the causes of the collapse of the Roman power. Otto Seeck has, I think, found no followers in his attempt to charge the third-century Roman emperors with the responsibility for that collapse. Through their continued *Ausrottung der Besten* — the persistent extermination of capacity and individual merit — the Caesars bred a terror of distinction and encouraged the spread of that slave mentality which issued logically and naturally in the triumph of Christianity — the Beggars' Religion — *die Religion des Betteltums*. An inverted Darwinism stamped out originality from the Empire: no man remained with the courage to be the master of his fate — the captain of his own soul. The way was open for "Byzantinismus," for crawling servility and fawning adulation of authority. Here the prejudice of one who was inspired by a passionate and life-long hatred of the Christian faith has, I cannot but feel, attempted to wrest history to its own purpose. Is there indeed any single century in the annals of the Empire which can show so many men of outstanding personality as can the fourth century of our era? Surely Professor Lot is not far from the truth when he exclaims: "If ever there were supermen in human history they are to be found in the Roman emperors of the third and fourth centuries" — men who shouldered the burden of a tottering world and resolutely refused to despair of the Republic. And beside the Roman emperors stand in the Christian camp such figures as Athansius and S. Basil in the East, as Ambrose and Augustine in the West. There is little of crawling servility in such men as these. The wonder of the fourth century to my mind is rather the heroic courage and the desperate resolution with which men strove to preserve that imperial organization which alone safeguarded the legacy of the ancient world. Further, you will not have failed to notice with what rigor Seeck presses the theory of the hereditary transmissibility of ἀρετή. So thoroughgoing a conviction might well rejoice the heart of a champion of an unreformed House of Lords. No, *Die Ausrottung der Besten* will not suffice to explain the decline of the Roman power.

Professor Tenney Frank, of the Johns Hopkins University, Baltimore, has approached the problem from another angle. From an elaborate statistical study of the Corpus of Latin inscriptions he concludes that Rome and the Latin West were flooded by an invasion of Greek and Oriental slaves: as these were emancipated and thus secured Roman citizenship the whole character of the citizen body was changed; on the basis of a consideration of some 13,900 sepulchral inscriptions he argues that nearly 90 percent of the Roman-born inhabitants of the Western capital were of foreign extraction. What lay behind and constantly reacted on those economic factors which have generally been adduced to explain the decline of the Roman power was the fact that those who had built Rome had given way to a different race. "The whole of Italy as well as the Romanized portions of Gaul and Spain were during the Empire dominated in blood by the East." In this fact Tenney Frank would find an explanation of the development from the Principate to the Dominate — the triumph of absolutism, of the spread of Oriental religions, the decline in Latin literature and the growing failure in that gift for the government of men which had built up the Empire.

But the foundations on which this far-reaching theory rests are not above suspicion. The nationality of Roman slaves is but rarely expressly stated in the sepulchral inscriptions, and thus it is upon the appearance of a Greek name for slave or freedman that Tenney Frank has inferred an Oriental origin. The legitimacy of this inference has been questioned by Miss Mary Gordon in her able study of the "Nationality of Slaves under the early Roman Empire," *JRS* xiv, 1924. A slave was a personal chattel, and slave-dealer or slave-owner could give to the slave any name which in his unfettered choice he might select: the slave dealers with whom Romans first came in contact were Greeks and thus, as Miss Gordon says, "Greek was the original language of the slave trade and this is reflected in servile nomenclature much as the use of French on modern menus and in the names affected by dressmakers suggests the history and associations of particular trades." In fact the nomenclature of the slave in the ancient world was scarcely less arbitrary than are the modern names given to our houses, our puddings, our horses or our dogs. An attempt to determine the domicile of origin of our cats or dogs solely by the names which their owners have given them would hardly be likely to produce results of high scientific value. The outlandish names of barbarian captives reduced to slavery would naturally be changed to more familiar forms, and Latin nomenclature was singularly poor and unimaginative: the Greek names were well known and resort to these was easy. It may be said that this reasoning is largely *a priori* and of little cogency. But Ettore Cicotti in a recent paper on "Motivi demografici e biologici nella rovina della civiltà antica" [Demographic and biological motifs in the ruins of the ancient civilization] in *Nuova Rivista storica* [New Historical Review], Anno xiv, fasc. i–ii, has adduced an interesting historical parallel. L. Livi (*La schiavitù domestica nei tempi di mezzo e nei moderni, Ricerche storiche di un antropologo* [Domestic slavery in middle and modern times: historical researches of an anthropologist], Roma, 1928) in 1928 published documents which his father copied from the State Archives of Florence. These documents record 357 sales of slaves: the transactions date from the years 1366 to 1390 — for the most part from the years 1366 to 1370. The majority of the slaves were of Tartar origin, though some were Greeks, Rumanians, etc. In these records the slave's original name is generally given and then follows the Italian name by which the slave is known. Thus the name of Lucia occurs forty-two times and represents such original names as Marchecta, Gingona, Erina, Minglacha, Saragosa, Casabai, Alterona and many others. Similarly the name of Caterina is given to slaves of Greek, Tartar, Turkish, Circassian, and Russian origin and has taken the place of such barbarous names as Coraghessan, Chrittias, Colcatalo, Tagaton, and Melich. The parallel is very instructive.

But this is not all: the sepulchral inscriptions studied by Tenney Frank extend over a period of three centuries: suppose that Rome had during the early Empire a population of some 800,000 with an annual mortality of 20 percent: in those three centuries the deaths would number 4.8 million. Tenney Frank has examined 13,900 inscriptions and those are derived from imperial and aristocratic *columbaria:* here the slaves would be better off and the percentage of accomplished foreign slaves would be higher: what of the nameless dead whom no record preserved, whose bodies lay in the vast common burial pits of the slave proletariat? These 13,900 dead who left permanent memorials behind them cannot be regarded as really representative of the general servile population of the city: we are not justified in using the percentage obtained from these records and applying it as though it were applicable to the whole class of slaves and of freedmen.

In the light of this criticism Tenney Frank's statistics are vitiated, and it must be admitted that the nationality of the slaves of Rome under the early Empire remains a matter of conjecture. There must have been a far greater number derived from Western Europe than are allowed for on Tenney Frank's calculations.

A somewhat different form of biological explanation is given by Professor Nilsson in his well-known book *Imperial Rome*. The most important problem for the Empire was that of race: that was decisive, for upon it depended the quality of Roman civilization. Culture rests on racial character. If the alien races and barbarian peoples were to be assimilated, they must be inter-penetrated by their conquerors. Since the Roman world was of vast extent and those of alien race were very numerous, an increase in the birth-rate of the Romans was required: instead of this the Roman birth-rate declined: the blood of the Romans became more and more diluted, and in place of the Romanization of the Empire a civilization of intercommunication and intercourse resulted in a mingling of races — an unchecked "mongrelization." Under the Empire cross-breeding, hybridization, spread throughout the provinces and in this widespread realm of mongrels all stable spiritual and moral standards were lost.

I confess that as soon as the word "race" is introduced into any discussion I realize that my only safe course lies in a resolute silence, for I have never been able to understand the precise significance of that ambiguous term. But when folk begin to ascribe all kinds of moral and spiritual failings to race-mixture it will hardly be expected that an Englishman will accept the insinuation without a protest. It is beyond calculation to estimate how many races and peoples have gone to his ethnological make-up, and he will not readily admit that the results of "mongrelization" have in his case been wholly deplorable. As an Englishman I am unlikely to discuss dispassionately the theory of Professor Nilsson. And unfortunately I am also a student of Byzantine history and as such I am convinced that the essential condition of the prosperity of the later Roman Empire was its possession of Asia Minor — that reservoir alike of money and of men. And Asia Minor of the Byzantines was surely man's most stupendous effort in race-mixture to which history can point: it was an ethnological museum. Professor Nilsson, to be quite frank, will have his work cut out to persuade an English Byzantinist that race-mixture is of necessity so poisonous and deadly a process. I had better leave it at that: you had best form your own judgment on the theory without further comment from me.

There still remains, however, the explanation of Professor Rostovtzeff as set forth in his *Social and Economic History of the Roman Empire*, a masterpiece for which any student of imperial Rome must have a sincere admiration. Professor Rostovtzeff's explanation of the collapse of the Roman power can be briefly summarized. It was through the medium of the *municipia* — of the towns — that Rome had unified Italy, and when she extended her conquests into the West of Europe she naturally favored the growths of towns as centers of Romanization. But the towns drew their wealth from the countryside, and the peasants bitterly resented this exploitation of their own class by the *bourgeoisie*. Under the peace of the Empire the civilian population became unfitted for the life of the military camps, and it was from the rude vigor of the peasantry that in the crisis of the third century the Roman armies were recruited. The peasant of the army made common cause with the peasant of the countryside and both waged a war of extermination against their oppressors of the city. The explanation of the downfall of the aristocracy and with them of the ancient civilization is thus to be found in a class-conscious alliance between the soldier and the worker on the land. Professor Rostovtzeff, it must be remembered, has seen in his native country an aristocratic regime overthrown by a similar alliance. And the only answer to this theory that I can give is quite simply that I can find no support for it in our extant sources. I have consulted every reference to the authorities cited by Professor Rostovtzeff and in my judgment none of them supports his reading of the facts. So far as I can see the constant terror of the peasants is the soldier: the last menace to a defaulting debtor is (according to the papyri) the creditor's threat: "I will send a soldier after you." The soldier is to the peasant what Napoleon or the policeman has been to successive generations of children in English nurseries. To the Roman peasant and soldier of the third century of our era there had not been granted a revelation of the gospel according to Karl Marx.

And thus I come back as a student of Byzantine history to the difficulty to which I referred at the beginning of this lecture. I believe that there was in Western Europe a break in the cultural development and that there was no corresponding break in the development of civilization in the Eastern provinces of the Roman Empire. To a Byzantinist, therefore, the problem which we are considering necessarily assumes a dual aspect: what he must discover, if he is to gain any intellectual satisfaction from the inquiry, is precisely the *differentia* which distinguishes the history of the Western provinces from that of the *partes orientales*. And so many of the modern explanations do not provide him with any such *differentia*. "Die Ausrottung der Besten," civil wars, and imperial jealousy of outstanding merit did not affect the West alone: the whole Roman world suffered from these scourges: the brutality of an undisciplined soldiery was likewise an evil common to both halves of the Empire. Soil-exhaustion, climatic change, these must have affected the entire Mediterranean area. The oppression of civil servants, the decay of the municipal senates, the flight from the land — all these ills the Eastern provinces were not spared. Greeks and Orientals invaded the West and we are told caused the collapse of the Roman power there; but in the East these same Greeks and Orientals sustained the Empire against unceasing assaults for another millennium: it seems mysterious. And therefore in closing it only remains for me to state the *differentia* as I see it and to suggest an explanation of this diversity in the history of East and West — an explanation which is so humiliatingly simple that I am constrained to believe that it must be right.

You realize then that I speak as a student of Byzantine history: a Byzantinist looks at the world of Western Europe. As I conceive of it, culture is essentially a social thing: it is born of intercourse and it needs a conscious solidarity of interest in order to sustain it. Roman civilization depended upon intercommunication, upon the influences radiating from the capital and returning to the capital for reinforcement. Such free communication, however, can be preserved only within an area which is safeguarded from violence: the Roman Empire was such an area safeguarded by the civil administration and by the frontier screen of the military forces. The civil service and the army together formed the steel framework which maintained the entire structure of civilization. It is perhaps with the Emperor Hadrian that one first observes a conscious realization of this function of the Roman power. The area of civilization is delimited on permanent lines: not expansion of territory, but concentration of resources in order to protect the solidarity of culture — that is the emperor's task. The barbarian invasions broke into this area of intercourse, and the establishment of barbarian kingdoms on Roman soil destroyed the single administration which was its counterpart. And the fatal significance of the establishment of these barbarian kingdoms lay in the fact that they withdrew from the Empire not only Roman soil, but also the revenues derived therefrom. Africa lost to the Vandals, Spain occupied by Sueve and Alan and Visigoth: Southern France a Visigothic kingdom and the rest of Gaul a battleground on which Aëtius fought and fought again: Italy alone remained as a source of revenue, and Italy was an impoverished land. The Western state was bankrupt. And the defense of the Empire demanded money, for Rome had so effectually provided the area of peaceful intercourse in Western Europe that her subjects were no longer soldiers: if battles were to be won they must be fought by barbarian mercenaries and for mercenaries to fight they must be paid. Further, Rome's effort in the West was a struggle with a double front: against the barbarian on land and against the Vandal fleet upon the sea. Rome possessed no technical superiority such as the invention of gunpowder might have given her, such as later the secret for the composition of the "Greek fire" gave to the Byzantine navy. Thus the tragedy of the Empire in the West lay precisely in the fact that she had not the wherewithal to keep at one and at the same time a mercenary army in the field and a fleet in commission. And the *differentia* which distinguishes the situation in the East of the Empire is in my judgment that, while the Danubian provinces were continuously ravaged, Asia Minor was for the most part untroubled by invasions: Asia Minor remained as I have said a reservoir alike of men and money. It was this reservoir which the West lacked. The West could throw no counterpoise into the scale against the supremacy of the barbarian; but the East amongst its own subjects numbered the hardy mountaineers — the Isaurians — and the fellow-countrymen of the Isaurian Tarasicodissa, whom history knows as the Emperor Zeno, could meet the menace of the barbarian mercenary and when the supremacy of the Alan Aspar had been broken, the Empire could send the Isaurian back to his mountains and Anastasius, an aged civilian who had only just escaped consecration as a bishop, could rule unchallenged. And as a consequence of the triumph of the civil power, the civil administration — the steel framework which maintained Byzantine civilization — was likewise preserved, and from the city of Constantine culture radiated and through intercourse with the capital was again reinforced. Here is preserved that conscious solidarity in the maintenance of civilization which guaranteed a real continuity. In the West there are survivals from the ancient world — true — a branch lopped from a tree may still produce shoots; but for all that the continuity of life is broken: the doom of decay is sure. Gregory of Tours is a remarkable man, but he is a lonely figure and he feels himself isolated. And against that figure I would set a scene at a Byzantine court — when the Emperor's barbarian mistress appeared in her radiant beauty at a reception, one courtier uttered the words **οὐ νέμεσις**: the barbarian queen did not understand the allusion, but for Byzantines the two words were enough to summon up the picture of Helen as she stood before the greybeards on the walls of Troy. So well did the aristocracy of East Rome know their Homer: such is the solidarity of Byzantine culture. In a word it was the pitiful poverty of Western Rome which crippled her in her effort to maintain that civil and military system which was the presupposition for the continued life of the ancient civilization.

Military Explanations

Edward N. Luttwak

A Failure of Strategy

Edward A. Luttwak was born in Arad, Transylvania, in 1942. He studied at the London School of Economics and at the Johns Hopkins University. He was a visiting professor at Johns Hopkins before joining the Center for Strategic and International Studies at Georgetown University, where he is now a research professor of international security affairs. He is also a defense consultant. Among his most important works are *Coup d'Etat* (1968), *The Political Uses of Sea Power* (1975), *The Israeli Army* (1975), *The Grand Strategy of the Soviet Union* (1983), and *The Pentagon and the Art of War: The Question of Military Reform* (1985).

VII Central Field Armies

If it were possible to create totally mobile military forces — that is, forces with a capacity for instant movement from place to place — then no part would ever have to be deployed forward at all. Instead, the entire force could be kept as a central reserve, without concern for ready availability and without regard for considerations of access or transit. On the other hand, if military forces are entirely immobile, the deployment scheme must make the best of individual unit locations in order to equalize the utility — tactical or political — of each forward deployment; and no forces should be kept in reserve at all, since immobile reserves can serve no purpose.

Not surprisingly, the strategy of imperial security that reached its culmination under Hadrian approximated the second of these two theoretical extremes. Even if their heavy equipment were carried by pack animals or in carts, the legions could not move any faster than a man could walk; in terms of the daily mileage of the Roman infantry, there-

Luttwak, Edward N. *The Grand Strategy of the Roman Empire: From the First Century A.D. to the Third*. The Johns Hopkins University Press, Baltimore/London, 1977, pp. 182–194.

fore, distances within the empire were immense. Since the frontiers *did* require the continuous presence of Roman forces to deter or defeat attacks, and since the enemies of the empire could not ordinarily coordinate their attacks, the deployment of a central reserve would have been a wasteful form of insurance: long delays would have intervened between the emergence of the threat and the arrival of redeployed forces. Better to keep all forces on the line and augment the defense of one sector by taking forces from another. Forces kept in reserve would serve no purpose and would cost as much as or more to maintain than forces in place and on duty. It is all very well to say that the Antonine deployment pattern was that of a thinly stretched line and to say that there was no mobile reserve ". . . *prête à voler au secours des points menacés.*" At the tactical level, auxiliary units and even legions could generally reach any threatened point of a provincial frontier in a matter of days, but a central reserve could hardly "fly"; it would have to march with agonizing slowness over a thousand miles or more to arrive at, say, the central Rhine sector from a central deployment point like Rome.

There is, nevertheless, one possible reason for the deployment of a centralized reserve even in a very low mobility environment: the protection of the central power itself. What might have been very inefficient from the point of view of the empire could have been very functional indeed for its ruler. Under the principate there was no central field force; there were only palace guards, private bodyguards, officer cadets in retinue, and the like: Augustus had his picked men (*evocati*) and his Batavian slave-guards; later, *speculatores* (select N.C.O.s) also appear in the retinue; and around the time of Domitian we find the *equites singulares*, a mounted force of perhaps 1,000 men. By the later third century the retinue came to include the *protectores*, seemingly a combined elite guard force and officer nursery. By 330 we find the *scholae*, an elite mounted force commanded, significantly, by the emperor rather than by the senior field officers (*magistri militum*), who controlled all the other central forces. In the *Notitia*, five units of *scholae* are listed in the West and seven in the East, probably of 500 men each. Private bodyguards often evolve into palace guards with official status, and there is a similar tendency on the part of elite military in the retinue to degenerate into ornamental palace guards. Another familiar pattern of evolution — palace guard to elite field force to field army — never developed in Rome, in spite of the fact that the

Praetorian cohorts were from the beginning a much more substantial force than any bodyguard could be.

Formed in 27 B.C. at the very beginning of the principate, the Praetorians were a privileged force receiving double the legionary salary, or 450 *denarii* per year. In his survey of the imperial forces, Tacitus lists nine Praetorian cohorts, but their number had increased to twelve by A.D. 47; one of the unsuccessful contenders of A.D. 69, Vitellius, further increased the number of cohorts to sixteen, but Vespasian reduced it again to nine. Finally, by 101 their number was increased once more to ten, resulting in a force of 5,000 troops, élite at least in status. In addition to the Praetorian cohorts there were also the Urban cohorts, always four in number and each 500 strong, and the *vigiles*, 3,500 strong by the end of the second century. But the latter were freedmen who served as firemen and policemen, and they cannot be counted as soldiers. Excluding the *vigiles*, there were thus a maximum of 8,000 men in organized units available as a central force. This was more than adequate to serve as a retinue to the emperor, but it certainly did not amount to a significant field force.

Even though there was a good deal of elasticity in the second-century system, it could not provide field armies for demanding campaigns. Hence, new legions had to be raised for major wars. Domitian raised the I *Minervia* for his war with the Chatti in 83, and Trajan had to raise the II *Traiana* and XXX *Ulpia* for his conquests; Antoninus Pius managed his not inconsiderable wars with expeditionary corps of auxiliary forces, but Marcus Aurelius was forced to form new legions (the II and III *Italicae*) to fight his northern wars. Beginning in 193, Septimius Severus fought a civil war of major proportions; almost immediately afterward he began a major Parthian war. Like his predecessors, he did so with an *ad hoc* field army of legionary *vexillationes* and auxiliaries; but he found, as his predecessors had, that this was not enough: by 196 three new legions, the I, II, and III *Parthicae*, were raised. No emperor since Augustus had raised as many.

Then came the major innovation: although the I and III *Parthicae* were duly posted on the newly conquered Mesopotamian frontier, in line with previous practice, the II *Parthica* was not. Instead, it was installed near Rome at Albanum, becoming the first legion to be regularly stationed anywhere in Italy since the inception of the principate. This, and the fact that all three Severan legions were placed under commanders of the equestrian class (*praefecti*) rather than of the senatorial class (*legati*), has suggested to both ancient and modern historians that the motive of the deployment of II *Parthica* was internal and political rather than external and military. This may have been so; but it is equally evident that the II *Parthica* could also have served as the nucleus of a central field army. The new legion on its own was already a substantial force, more so than the total establishment of pre-Severan Praetorians, Urban cohorts, and *Equites Singulares*. But Severus increased substantially these forces: each Praetorian cohort was doubled in size to 1,000 men, for a total of 10,000; the Urban cohorts were tripled to 1,500 men each, for a total of 6,000; and even the number of *vigiles* was doubled to 7,000. Only the number of the *Equites Singulares* failed to increase. There were, in addition, some troops, especially cavalry, attached to the obscure *Castra Peregrina*, an institution akin to an imperial G.H.Q.

It is unfortunate that no coherent picture of the subsequent employment of these forces can be gleaned from the inadequate sources, but it is certain that out of the 30,000 men now permanently available in Rome and free of frontier-defense duties, a substantial central reserve could be extracted for actual campaigning, perhaps as many as 23,000 men — the equivalent of almost four legions. This was a significant force: Marcus Aurelius took three legions with him to fight Parthia, and their absence from the frontiers may have triggered the dangerous northern wars of his reign.

It is in the most difficult years of the third century, under Gallienus (253–68), that we hear of a new central reserve, or rather, regional field reserves: these were cavalry forces deployed on major road axes such as Aquileia (controlling the major eastern gateway into Italy), Sirmium for the mid-Danube sector, Poetovio in the Drava valley, and Lychnidus on the major highway into Greece from the north. On the basis of the scattered evidence we have, the outlines of a new strategy emerge: a defense-in-depth so deep that it is virtually an elastic defense in which nothing but the Italian core is securely held.

The major instrument of this strategy was a wholly mobile cavalry corps, which appears to have been constituted by Gallienus, or at least increased by him. Aureolus served for ten years as its commander, fighting loyally against both internal and external enemies before finally turning against Gallienus in 268; the usurpation failed, but Gallienus was assassinated while besieging Milan, where the defeated Aureolus was seeking refuge. Significantly, his designated successor was another cavalry commander, Claudius, who was to rule for two years (268–70), winning great victories. Claudius, in turn, was succeeded by another and much greater cavalry commander, Aurelian, who ruled until his murder in 275. Clearly, the existence of a mobile corps of cavalry unattached to any fixed position had great political significance: if its commander were not the emperor himself, he could become emperor, since there was no comparable force that could be brought to bear against a large, centralized cavalry corps.

Very little is known of the composition of this cavalry. It included units of *promoti* (which may have been the old 120-horse legionary cavalry contingents), as well as units of native cavalry (*equites Dalmatae* and *equites Mauri*) and possibly some heavy cavalry (*Scutarii*). It is also possible that under Gallienus the legions were given new cavalry contingents of 726 men in place of the original 120. It was at this time that the term *vexillatio* underwent its change of meaning, for it appears in 269 with its original meaning of a legionary *infantry* detachment, but by 293 it denotes a cavalry unit. The term must have initially connoted a mobile field unit *par excellence*, and it is easy to see the transformation taking place as the importance of the cavalry increases. In the celebrations of the tenth year of Gallienus's rule the new importance of the cavalry was given formal recognition: in the ritual hierarchy of the procession, it was given the same status as the Praetorian Guard.

The cavalry doubled the strategic mobility of Roman expeditionary forces moving overland (ca. fifty miles per day against ca. twenty-five), but this strategic advantage entailed a tactical disadvantage: when the Roman soldier became a cavalryman he could retain no trace of his former tactical superiority. Roman cavalry fought the barbarians without the inherent advantage enjoyed by even a decadent legionary. Perhaps it is for this reason that the sources of the nostalgic Vegetius were hostile to the cavalry, arguing that the infantry was cheaper, more versatile, and more appropriate as a vehicle of legionary traditions.

The history of the Roman cavalry records the consistent success of large bodies of light cavalry armed with missile weapons and the equally consistent failure of the heavy cavalry equipped with shock weapons. Nevertheless, under Trajan a milliary unit of heavy lancers (*Ala I Ulpia Contariorum Miliaria*) had already appeared; and even earlier, Josephus had described a weapon of Vespasian's cavalry in Judea (ca. 68) as a *kontos*, i.e., a heavy lance, the characteristic weapon of the heavy cavalry. This cavalry had no body armor; however, the first unit of *armored* cavalry appears in Hadrian's time, with an *Ala I Gallorum et Pannoniorum Catafractata*, a designation that describes mailed cavalry with little rigid armor. The heavy cavalry had been the leading force of the Parthians, and it was also the leading force of the Sassanid armies. But their heavy cavalry was fully protected with rigid armor, and the horses were partly armored as well, in the familiar manner of late-medieval knights. Roman troops nicknamed them *clibanarii* (bread-ovens), and they certainly could not have had an easy time of it in the heat of the Syrian desert.

Late in 271, Aurelian sailed east to destroy the power of Palmyra with a force of legionary detachments, Praetorian cohorts, and above all, light cavalry of Moorish and Dalmatian origin. First by the Orontes River and then at Emesa, Aurelian soundly defeated the Palmyrans, using the same tactic on both occasions: the light and unencumbered native horse retreated and the enemy *clibanarii* pursued — until they were exhausted. Then the real fighting began. Later, when Persian forces intervened to take the Romans besieging Palmyra in the flank, they were defeated in turn with the same tactics. In spite of this ample demonstration of the superiority of light cavalry over armored horsemen *if supported by steady infantry*, units of *clibanarii* began to appear in the Roman army: nine are listed in the *Notitia Dignitatum*, including a unit described as *equites sagittarii clibanarii* (i.e., armored mounted archers) — most likely a decorative but ineffectual combination of light weaponry and heavy armor. The combat record of this armored cavalry was dismal.

There was no room for an unattached cavalry corps in Diocletian's scheme of shallow defense-in-depth. Strategically, it had been the natural instrument of an "elastic defense," while on the political level its very existence was destabilizing. But Diocletian did not need to dissolve the cavalry corps, for it had probably already disappeared. It remains uncertain whether the Moorish and Dalmatian *equites* were disbanded by Aurelian after his victory over Palmyra in order to garrison the disorganized eastern frontiers — or whether Diocletian himself disbanded them. The *promoti* may have been attached to the legions once again, though the link may have been only administrative.

The question of the deployment of the cavalry under Diocletian is directly connected with a broader, more important, and much more controversial issue — the deployment of a field army as such. The orthodox view has been that Diocletian and his colleagues created or expanded the *sacer comitatus* (i.e., the field escort of the emperors), replacing the improvised field forces of their predecessors with standing field armies and creating the dual structure of static border troops *limitanei)* and field forces *(comitatenses)* that characterized the army of the late empire. According to this approach, Constantine merely perfected the change by adding a command structure a generation later. The *sacer comitatus* would thus have amounted to a field army and would have been much more than a bodyguard, since (1) it was of substantial size, and (2) it was not uniform in composition, as the old Praetorian cohorts had been. It included the latter, whose number was, however, reduced; *lanciarii*, elite infantry selected from the legions, cavalry units, called *comites*; the prestigious Moorish cavalry; select new legions (*Ioviani* and *Herculiani*); and possibly cavalry *promoti*.

In the other, less traditional view, which was advanced earlier in the century and then rejected, the argument was that the *sacer comitatus* was nothing more than the traditional escort of the emperors and not a field army or even the nucleus of one. It was held that Diocletian had expanded the army, doubling it in size, but it was Constantine who had removed large numbers of troops from the frontier sectors to form his central field force of *comitatenses*. Recently restated in a monographic study of considerable authority, which has been criticized but also authoritatively accepted, at least in great part, this view now seems persuasive. The controversy over the authorship of the reform is still unresolved, for doubts on subordinate but important questions remain. There is no doubt, however, that it was Constantine who created the new commands of the standing field army, the *magister peditum* of the infantry and the *magister equitum* of the cavalry.

In any event, by the first decades of the fourth century the dual army structure was in existence, with *limitanei* and provincial troops on the border under the control of sector commanders (*duces*), and with centralized field forces under the emperor and his *magistri*. The subsequent evolution of the dual army structure was predictable. In the *Notitia*, there are forty-eight legions listed as *pseudocomitatenses*, indicating that they were transferred into the field army after having served as provincial forces. When Constantine formed, or at least enlarged, his field army, he did raise some new units, including the *auxilia*, but he must also have considerably weakened the provincial forces in order to augment his field forces. This was no doubt the transfer of troops from the frontiers to the cities that the fifth century

historian, Zosimus, however prejudiced by his anti-Christian sentiments, rightly criticized. It is probable that during the late fourth century the *comitatenses* grew steadily in size at the expense of the provincial forces (now all called *limitanei*), whose relative status and privileges continued to decline.

VIII Conclusion

It is apparent that reductions made in the provincial forces that guarded the frontiers in order to strengthen the central field armies would always serve to provide political security for the imperial power, but they must inevitably have downgraded the day-to-day security of the common people. In the very late stages of imperial devolution in the West, it is not unusual to find the frontiers stripped wholesale of their remaining garrisons to augment central field forces, as happened in 406 under Stilicho, who was engaging in internal warfare. In such cases, the frontier was seemingly left to be "defended" by barbarian alliances, which were hollow versions of the client relationships of the first century. Such alliances were rented, not bought; inducements could provide no security once the indispensable element of deterrence was gone.

The lists of the *Notitia Dignitatum*, whatever their exact date, give some notion of the distribution of forces between the frontier sectors and the field armies, and several attempts have been made to quantify the distribution on the basis of varying estimates of unit sizes. (See Table 1.)

These estimates, so widely different in authority and reasoning (they reflect, *inter alia*, different datings of the *Notitia*) have one thing in common: in each case the percentage of *limitanei* is a substantially higher figure for the East, which survived the fifth century crisis, than for the West, which did not. The implication is obvious, and so is its relationship to the argument made here as to the strategic worth of reserve forces in a very low mobility environment. The fact that the enemies of the empire could not have been significantly more mobile is irrelevant. Since the external threat was uncoordinated, *relative* mobility was unimportant. What mattered was the *absolute* mobility of Roman forces deployed in the rear, which was much too low to justify the dual system on military grounds.

Septimius Severus commanded his armies against both internal and external enemies in both East and West once he became emperor,

TABLE 1 **Distribution of Troops: Frontiers and Field Armies in the East and West**

	Number of Troops				
	(1)	(2)	(3)	(4)	(5)
Western *comitatus*	—	111,000	113,000	123,800	94,000
Eastern *comitatus*	—	94,500	104,000	96,300	79,000
Total *comitatenses*	194,500	205,500	217,000	220,100	173,000
Western *limitanei*	—	200,000	135,000	138,000	122,000/130,000
Eastern *limitanei*	—	332,000	248,000	165,700	201,500
Total *limitanei*	360,000	532,000	383,000	303,700	323,500/331,500
Total Western	—	311,000	248,000	261,800	226,000/224,000
Total Eastern	—	426,500	352,000	262,000	280,500
Percentage of *limitanei* in West	—	64%	54%	47%	56–58%
Percentage of *limitanei* in East	—	78%	70%	63%	72%
Total Troops, East and West	554,500	737,500	600,000	523,800	496,500/504,500
Percentage of *limitanei* in total	65%	72%	64%	58%	65% –

Source: (1) T. Mommsen, "Das römische Militärwesen seit Diocletian," *Hermes* 24 (1889): 263 cited in Clemente, *La Notitia Dignitatum*, p. 156, n. 71; (2) Nischer, "Army Reforms of Diocletian and Constantine," p. 54; (3) Jones, *Later Roman Empire*, vol. 3, table 15, pp. 379–80; (4) Várady, "New Evidences on Some Problems of Late Roman Military Organization," p. 360; (5) J. Szilágyi, "Les Variations des centres de préponderance militaire dans les provinces frontières de l'empire romain," *Acta Antiqua Academiae Scientarum Hungaricae* 2(1953): 217.

even though he had no experience of active duty until he came to power. Again the implication is clear: "The example of Severus became a rule to which there could be no exceptions. The emperor must command his armies in the field, whatever his age or his personal inclinations — and if he was unsuccessful, a better general would be put in his place." The field armies of the later empire were much larger than those of the principate, but even when distributed in regional reserves the *comitatenses* could not hope to have adequate strategic mobility to defend imperial territory preclusively: the enemy could be intercepted and often defeated, but only after he had done his worst. On the other hand, the centralized field armies could serve to protect the power of the soldier-emperors who controlled them, and this was the one task that the field armies continued to perform effectively until the very end.

But the damage inflicted upon imperial territories, private lives, and private property was cumulative; it relentlessly eroded the logistic base of the empire and relentlessly diminished the worth of the imperial structure to its subjects.

Epilogue
The Three Systems: An Evaluation

From the Constantinian version of defense-in-depth, with its dual structure of border troops and central field units, the stratification of the imperial army predictably evolved further. By the later fourth century, we find new units, styled *palatini*, serving as the central field forces, under the direct command of the emperors of East and West; the *comitatenses* have become lower-status *regional* field armies, while the *limitanei* have sunk still lower in relative status. It may safely be assumed that this evolution caused a further reduction in the quality and quantity of the human and material resources available for territorial defense, both local and regional. Other things being equal, it must have entailed a further decline in territorial security, with all its logistic and societal consequences, manifest in the increasing weakness of the empire.

A triple deployment in depth would of course be much more

resilient than any linear deployment, but this "resilience" could merely mean that the central power could thereby survive for another season of tax gathering from a population now constantly exposed to the violence of endemic warfare and the ravages of unopposed barbarian incursions. Finally, the situation could so deteriorate that in the fifth century an ordinary citizen of the empire, a merchant from Viminacium, could prefer life outside the empire, finding a desirable new home among a people no gentler than the Huns, in the very camp of Attila.

Let us then reconsider the three systems of imperial security. First was the system described here as Julio-Claudian, but more properly perhaps to be thought of as the system of the republican empire. Around its core areas the empire was hegemonic in nature, with client states autonomously responsible for implementing Roman *desiderata* and providing out of their own resources, and through their obedience, for the territorial security of the core areas. No Roman troops are ordinarily deployed in the client states or with client tribes, but the stability of the system requires a constant diplomatic effort both to ensure that each client will be continually aware of the totality of Roman power (while being itself politically isolated) and to maintain the internal (e.g., dynastic) and regional (i.e., inter-client) equilibrium of the client structure. Client states great and small are thus kept in subjection by their own perceptions of Roman power, and this deterrent force was complemented by positive inducements, notably subsidies.

Under this system, the armed forces that the clients perceive as an undivided force of overwhelming strength are actually distributed in a vast circle around Rome. But these troops are still concentrated in multi-legion armies and are not committed to territorial defense, so they are inherently mobile and freely redeployable. The flexibility of the force structure is such that almost half the army can be sent to a single rebellious province (Illyricum in A.D. 6–9), without prejudicing the security of the rest of the empire. In the absence of such rebellions, this flexibility results in vast "disposable" military strength, which can be used for further expansion where the front remains "open," as in Germany before A.D. 9 or Britain under Claudius.

Owing to its hegemonic nature, the sphere of imperial control is limited only by the range at which others perceive Roman power as compelling obedience. The reach of Roman power and the costs of its military forces need not, therefore, be proportional. Further extensions of the empire, in a hegemonic mode, do not require increases in the military forces maintained. New clients added to the empire will respond to the same compulsion as have all the clients brought within the sphere of imperial control before them. Hence the economy of force of the Julio-Claudian system, and its efficiency. But this was a system whose goal was to enhance the security of Roman control rather than the security of the imperial territory and its populations.

The Antonine system, in use in one form or another from the Flavian era after A.D. 69 to the crisis of the mid-third century, reflects the territorialization of the empire and the reorientation of its priorities. Armed forces are now everywhere deployed to secure the tranquillity and, therefore, the prosperity of border lands and, *a fortiori*, of the interior. The military strength of the empire and its effective power are now rigidly proportional, since this strength is now largely used directly, not as a tool of political suasion. Clients remain, but they are much less useful than in the past: the task of maintaining territorial security is efficiently shifted from weak clients to widely distributed frontier forces, while strong clients can no longer be tolerated, since their strength may now dangerously exceed that of the adjacent imperial forces.

Nevertheless, the empire remains strong, and not the least of its strength is political. A real growing prosperity and a voluntary Romanization are eliminating the last vestiges of nativistic disaffection and creating a strong base of support for the unitary regime. Facing enemies widely separated from one another at the periphery, the empire can still send overwhelmingly powerful forces against them, since the tranquillity of the provinces — and, in places, elaborate border-defense infrastructures — allow peace to be temporarily maintained even with much-depleted frontier forces. This residual offensive capability is primarily useful as a diplomatic instrument, its latent threat serving to keep the neighbors of the empire divided — if not necessarily obedient.

Nevertheless, the cultural and economic influence of Rome on the lives of all the neighbors of the empire is itself creating a cultural and political basis for common action against it. Men who had nothing in common now acquire elements of a culture shared by all but belonging to none. Beyond the Rhine, the federation of border peoples that will turn them into formidable multi-tribal agglomerations is beginning. Opposed by the relentless force of cultural transformation,

Roman diplomacy becomes less effective in keeping the enemies of the empire divided. And the system of perimeter defense, keyed to *low-intensity* threats, cannot adequately contend with their unity.

The third system arose in response to this intractable combination of diplomatic and military problems whose consequences became manifest in the great crisis of the third century. Under Diocletian, a shallow and structured defense-in-depth replaces the "elastic defense" of Gallienus and the previous generation, in which *ad hoc* field armies had fought agglomerations of barbarians deep within imperial territory.

Like the Antonine, the new system provides no disposable surplus of military power either for offensive use or for diplomatic coercion, deterrent, or compellent. The difference is that the third system no longer has a "surge" capability either, since the enemies of the empire are no longer kept on the defensive by forward defense tactics; instead, they are only contained. When the containment forces are reduced to muster *ad hoc* field forces, penetrations occur, and the Antonine remnants of a capacity to generate the image of power for the purposes of political suasion is irrevocably lost. It follows that diplomatic relationships with external powers must now reflect the local balance of forces — which cannot always favor the empire on every sector of the perimeter.

With this, the output and input of the system are finally equated. The level of security provided becomes directly proportional to the amount of the resources expended on the army and on frontier fortifications. The great economy of force that made the unitary empire a most efficient provider of security is lost. From now on it merely enjoys certain modest economies of scale over the alternative of independent regional states. And these economies of scale are not large enough to compensate for much administrative inefficiency or venality. In the end, the idea and the reality of the unitary empire is sustained no longer by the logic of collective security, but only by the will of those who control the imperial power, and by men's fear of the unknown.

Arther Ferrill

A Failure of Tactics

Arther Ferrill was born in Enid, Oklahoma, in 1938. He was educated at Wichita State University and the University of Illinois. Since 1964 he has been at the University of Washington, where he is now Professor of History. His most important works are *The Origins of War: From the Stone Age to Alexander the Great* (1985) and *The Fall of the Roman Empire: The Military Explanation* (1986). He is currently working on a biography of the Roman emperor Caligula.

The Fall of Rome

When the adherents of the "Late Antique" school use the word "transformation" in describing the fall of Rome, they mean it as an explanation as well as a description. The transformation they see from Rome to the Middle Ages developed over centuries, not years. Yet the fall of Rome in the West was more than a process — it was also an event, one that occurred rather suddenly, in the same sense at least in which the fall of the British Empire after World War II required about a generation but can nevertheless be said to have been sudden.

If one takes 476 as the date of the fall, and looks back merely a hundred years to 376, one can see an empire still strong, still as large as the Empire of Augustus, still respected by its foes across the imperial frontiers. Furthermore, it was defended by an army that continued to fight effectively despite the catastrophe in Persia under Julian, a strategic blow that cannot be laid at the feet of the legions.

On the other hand, 376 was itself an important year in Roman history. It was then that the Visigoths, driven by the pressure of the Huns and the Ostrogoths, crossed the Danube with the emperor's permission to settle permanently in Roman territory. Thus began a series of invasions (for the crossing of the Danube soon turned into an invasion) that led in a hundred years to the fall of the Western Roman

From *The Fall of the Roman Empire: A Military Explanation* by Arther Ferrill, 1986. Reprinted by permission of Thames and Hudson Ltd., London.

Empire. It is easy with hindsight to regard that fall as inevitable, to emphasize the vulnerability and fragility of the Roman Empire, to see in the fall of Rome what has been called, in another context, "the weary Titan syndrome." One cannot argue, as in the case of modern Britain, that the loss of empire "cushioned" Rome's fall in the world. The Empire had been so inextricably identified with Rome itself that the fall of the Empire *was* the fall of Rome.

To see Roman history from Marcus Aurelius on, as the story of a troubled giant, as so many historians do, a decaying empire, the victim of "cultural and world-political Angst," is to miss the point. Some historians, recognizing the common fallacy, turn the problem around and ask why the Empire survived so long. Both tendencies, however, have the same effect — to direct attention away from a consideration of the factors that led to the disappearance of the Western Roman Empire in the last half of the fifth century; one by seeking the causes in the much too distant past and the other by accepting the fact as inevitable.

The Roman Empire on the eve of Adrianople was not obviously on a downhill course. Nor had Roman citizens lost faith in their destiny to rule the world. The Empire was strong, despite a recent defeat in Persia, and it continued to show remarkable strength in the devastating thirty or so years between the defeat at Adrianople and the sack of Rome by Alaric. Since the days of the Punic Wars the strategic strength of Rome had consisted to a certain extent in the ability of the Empire to suffer tactical defeats in the field and yet mobilize new forces to continue the fighting.

Even after A.D. 410 some of that resilience remained, but there was one difference, particularly in the West. Rome had almost stopped producing its own soldiers, and those it did draw into military service were no longer trained in the ancient tactics of close-order formation though they tried to fight that way. Many historians have argued, either directly or more often by emphasizing other causes, that the fall of Rome was not primarily a military phenomenon. In fact, it was exactly that. After 410 the emperor in the West could no longer project military power to the ancient frontiers. That weakness led immediately to the loss of Britain and within a generation to the loss of Africa. One need not produce a string of decisive battles in order to demonstrate a military collapse. The shrinkage of the imperial frontiers from 410 to 440 was directly the result of military conquests by barbarian forces. To be sure, the loss of strategic resources in money, material and manpower compounded the mere loss of territory and made military defence of the remainder of the Empire even more difficult. It is simply perverse, however, to argue that Rome's strategic problems in the 440s, 50s and 60s were primarily the result of financial and political difficulties or of long-term trends such as gradual depopulation.

The modern historian must keep in mind the fact that Rome in the East did not fall, and any explanation of the fall of Rome must also account for its survival in Byzantium. Why was the East able to marshal its military resources, to survive the barbarian invasions and to emerge under Justinian in the sixth century with a burst of military power sufficient to reconquer, at least temporarily, parts of the West? Some specifically military explanations can be set aside. Recruitment in the Late Empire was difficult, but too much has been made of imperial legislation on that score. Even in the great days of the Roman Empire, for example in the last years of Augustus, recruitment could be a problem during military crises. In the fourth and fifth centuries it was no greater a problem in the West than in the East, at least not until western difficulties were highly exacerbated by military and territorial losses. The strategic strength of the East behind the impenetrable wall of Constantinople is often emphasized as a factor in the survival of the Byzantine Empire, but one must look also at the elements of weakness in the West.

In fact, of course, the sack of Rome, the loss of Britain and of Africa, and parts of Gaul and Spain, dealt heavy blows to the military capacity of the Western emperor. If one begins the story of Rome's fall with the year 440, the collapse of the West and not of the East is easy enough to explain. By 440 western forces were much weaker than those of the East. That was not true, however, on the last day of the year 406, the day Vandals, Suebi and Alamanni crossed the frozen Rhine and moved into Gaul. In 406, on paper, western power was as great as eastern. Stilicho had driven Alaric and Radagaisus out of Italy. Indeed on behalf of the West he had dealt more effectively with Alaric than eastern generals had done. Yet in the short period, 407–10, the West received an ultimately fatal blow. After 410 it was never again militarily as strong as the East. Barbarians were permanently established in Gaul and Spain, and Britain had been lost.

One could argue, as I am inclined to do, that even after 410 the emperor of the West had not lost all military options, that he might yet have restored Roman military power, if not in Britain, at least in the rest of the Western Empire. But military losses in 407–10 were sufficient to make a major difference between the strategic, projective military power of the Eastern and Western emperors. Those few years constitute a turning point after which it is no longer necessary to explain why the West fell and the East survived.

Why, then, did the West do so badly in 407–10? To a certain extent, as we have seen, the strategic strength of the East contributed to the fall of the West. Constantinople was heavily defended. No barbarian tribe could possibly hope to storm those walls. Furthermore, the emperor in the East was better able to afford the heavy subsidies barbarian leaders demanded in the years after Adrianople, though in fact the West also paid a heavy monetary price for peace.

Perhaps the most popular approach to the explanation of Rome's fall, if we can set aside the examination of those long-term causes such as depopulation, race mixture, political and economic deterioration, lead poisoning and other fashionable theories, has been to find a scapegoat, to see in an error or errors of human judgment the fatal mistake that caused the tragedy. Although this approach has often been ridiculed in recent times, it is not without merit. Leaders do matter. Strategic decisions produce successful or unsuccessful results. The weight of history, in the form of long-term trends, may impose limitations on the military mind, but a good general or political leader will bear the burden and solve his strategic problems one way or another.

The Emperor Honorius has been asked by ancient and modern historians alike to take far too much of the blame for Rome's fall. Partly that is because Rome suffered its great humiliation in 407–10 under his rule, and since he did not prevent it, he must undoubtedly be held responsible for it. As citizens we apply this kind of standard to our present leaders, and it is perhaps not unreasonable to do the same for leaders of the past. On the other hand, if it is possible to be right and still lose, Honorius may have done just that. He does not deserve the criticism he uniformly gets for doing nothing, since doing nothing was almost certainly, for him, an "active" or conscious strategy, not simply negligence, a strategy that might in fact have worked if someone had not opened a gate to Rome for Alaric's Visigoths in August 410.

Stilicho's role in the fall of the West is harder to assess, and he has had vigorous attackers and defenders. That he was much too interested in affairs in Constantinople rather than in Italy is certain.

Whether he can also be accused of having let Alaric escape on several occasions when the barbarian leader might have been crushed is impossible to determine on the basis of the inadequate surviving evidence. To those who see the fall of Rome as a matter of trends, Stilicho's efforts are of no concern. Presumably if he had not left Alaric free to sack Rome, someone else would have sacked it. How can even Rome fight trends? But in fact the fate of the Western Roman Empire might have been very different had events in 407–10 taken another course. Insofar as human agency might have prevented them, the failure of Stilicho is significant. His inability to shape a better future for the Western Roman Empire was much more the result of actual mistaken judgment (leading to his execution in 408) than was the failure of Honorius. Stilicho was wrong; Honorius was unlucky.

It is also true, however, that the army itself underwent significant deterioration between 378 and 410, more so in the West than in the East. In the fourth century the western army had been the better one. It was the eastern army that had been defeated in Persia and at Adrianople, but at the Frigid River in 394 Theodosius had beaten the western army with the help of twenty thousand Visigoths, who attacked Arbogast and Eugenius in line of column suffering extraordinarily heavy losses (50 per cent). The loss at the Frigidus undoubtedly demoralized the western army to a certain extent, but it must have been much more humiliated by its treatment at the hands of Stilicho, who commanded it from 395 to 408.

At that time there was a reaction in the East against the use of Germans in the Roman army, but in the West Stilicho imposed the Theodosian policy of barbarization. First, with the western army in the Balkans he failed to crush Alaric on at least two occasions, and then, during the successful campaigns in Italy from 401 to 405 against Alaric (who got away again, twice) and Radagaisus, Stilicho relied heavily on barbarian troops. His use of barbarians became a matter of controversy and contributed to his downfall in 408. For that reason "barbarization" in this period is often treated as a political problem (which it was), and little consideration has been given to the probable effect the policy had on the proud army of the West.

There is no way of knowing, unfortunately, to what extent the central, mobile army in Italy, by 408, was a traditional Roman army and to what extent it had become overwhelmed by barbarian influences. Possibly, if the resources of Britain and Gaul had been united with the army of Italy in the crisis of 408–10, it might have been possible to have defeated Alaric again, but the revolt of Constantine prevented that kind of cooperation, and Honorius decided to pursue a strategy of exhaustion rather than to bring Alaric to battle. Such a policy was extremely humiliating for the army. General Sir John Hackett has said: "An army's good qualities are best shown when it is losing." To fight on in the face of certain defeat requires much more than courage. But the army of the West in the crisis of 408–10 was not allowed to fight at all, and after what it had suffered earlier at the hands of Stilicho, this was the crushing blow. Never again was the emperor of the West the military equal of his eastern counterpart.

In the aftermath of 410 Constantius and Aëtius had done the best they could to maintain Rome's reduced position in the West. Constantius was the better strategist of the two, and his skilful use of naval power did give the regime, now in Ravenna, a new lease of life. Aëtius was unfortunately too interested in Gaul at the expense of Italy, Spain and particularly Africa. The loss of Carthage was a double blow to Rome since the emperor in the West had relied heavily on African grain and because the resources of the African city now strengthened the Vandal kingdom. Declining revenues and territory made recruitment difficult, and the true Roman contingent of the army that fought Attila at Châlons was the object of ridicule. In the last twenty years of the Western Empire, after the death of Valentinian III, the central government in Italy relied exclusively on barbarians until the latter finally, in 476, put one of their own officers in as king and abolished the emperorship in the West.

It is clear that after 410 the Roman army no longer had any special advantage, tactically, over barbarian armies — simply because the Roman army had been barbarized. Hans Delbrück has argued that Roman strength had always been strategic rather than tactical, that man for man Roman armies were no better than Germanic ones:

> *Vis-a-vis civilized peoples, barbarians have the advantage of having at their disposal the warlike power of unbridled animal instincts, of basic toughness. Civilization refines the human being, makes him more sensitive, and in doing so it decreases his military worth, not only his bodily strength but also his physical courage.*

Delbrück goes on to say that Roman tactical organization and training merely "equalized the situation."

This is stuff and nonsense, as careful reading of du Picq might have revealed. Rome's army had always been small, relative to the population of the Empire, because Roman training and discipline gave it an unparalleled advantage in tactically effective, close-order formation. By 451, to judge from the speech Attila gave to the Huns at the battle of Châlons, the feeble remnant of the once-proud legions still fought in the ancient formation, but apparently without the training and discipline. Without them, close order was worse than no order at all. Romans could be expected to huddle behind their screen of shields; Visigoths and Alans would do the fighting. As the western army became barbarized, it lost its tactical superiority, and Rome fell to the onrush of barbarism.

The Emperor Justinian, his ministers and guards (527–565). This 6th century mosaic from Ravenna shows the Emperor Justinian among his ministers and guards. During his reign the Eastern Roman Empire based at Constantinople flourished and expanded. (Alinari/Art Resource)

PART

Decline, Transformation, or Fall

Peter Brown

Geographical Transformation

Peter Brown was born in Dublin in 1935. He received his MA at New College, Oxford, and was a Harmsworth Senior Scholar at Merton College, Oxford, a Prize Fellow at All Souls College, Oxford, a Junior Research Fellow, a Senior Research Fellow, and a Fellow at All Souls College. He has been a Lecturer in Medieval History at Merton College, Oxford, a Special Lecturer in late Roman and early Byzantine History, and a Reader at the University of Oxford. His publications include *Augustine of Hippo*, *The World of Late Antiquity*, and *Religion and Society in the Age of St. Augustine*.

From *The World of Late Antiquity* by Peter Brown, 1971. Reprinted by permission of Thames and Hudson Ltd., London.

This book [*The World of Late Antiquity*] is a study of social and cultural change. I hope that the reader will put it down with some idea of how, and even of why, the Late Antique world (in the period from about A.D. 200 to about 700) came to differ from "classical" civilization, and of how the headlong changes of this period, in turn, determined the varying evolution of western Europe, of eastern Europe and of the Near East.

To study such a period one must be constantly aware of the tension between change and continuity in the exceptionally ancient and well-rooted world around the Mediterranean. On the one hand, this is notoriously the time when certain ancient institutions, whose absence would have seemed quite unimaginable to a man of about A.D. 250, irrevocably disappeared. By 476, the Roman Empire had vanished from western Europe; by 655, the Persian Empire had vanished from the Near East. It is only too easy to write about the Late Antique world as if it were merely a melancholy tale of "Decline and Fall": of the end of the Roman Empire as viewed from the West; of the Persian, Sassanian empire, as viewed from Iran. On the other hand, we are increasingly aware of the astounding new beginnings associated with this period: we go to it to discover why Europe became Christian and why the Near East became Muslim; we have become extremely sensitive to the "contemporary" quality of the new, abstract art of this age; the writings of men like Plotinus and Augustine surprise us, as we catch strains — as in some unaccustomed overture — of so much that a sensitive European has come to regard as most "modern" and valuable in his own culture.

Looking at the Late Antique world, we are caught between the regretful contemplation of ancient ruins and the excited acclamation of new growth. What we often lack is a sense of what it was like to live in that world. Like many contemporaries of the changes we shall read about, we become either extreme conservatives or hysterical radicals. A Roman senator could write as if he still lived in the days of Augustus, and wake up, as many did at the end of the fifth century A.D., to realize that there was no longer a Roman emperor in Italy. Again, a Christian bishop might welcome the disasters of the barbarian invasions, as if they had turned men irrevocably from earthly civilization to the Heavenly Jerusalem, yet he will do this in a Latin or a Greek unself-consciously modeled on the ancient classics; and he will betray attitudes to the universe, prejudices and patterns of behavior that mark him out as a man still firmly rooted in eight hundred years of Mediterranean life.

How to draw on a great past without smothering change. How to change without losing one's roots. Above all, what to do with the stranger in one's midst — with men excluded in a traditionally aristocratic society, with thoughts denied expression by a traditional culture, with needs not articulated in conventional religion, with the utter foreigner from across the frontier. These are the problems which every civilized society has had to face. They were particularly insistent in the Late Antique period. I do not imagine that a reader can be so untouched by the idea of classical Greece and Rome or so indifferent to the influence of Christianity, as not to wish to come to some judgment on the Late Antique world that saw the radical transformation of the one and the victory over classical paganism of the other. But I should make it plain that, in presenting the evidence, I have concentrated on the manner in which the men of the Late Antique world faced the problem of change.

The Roman Empire covered a vast and diverse territory: the changes it experienced in this period were complex and various. They range from obvious and well-documented developments, such as the repercussions of war and high taxation on the society of the third and fourth centuries, to shifts as intimate and mysterious as those that affected men's relations to their own body and to their immediate neighbors. I trust that the reader will bear with me, therefore, if I begin the first part of this book with three chapters that sketch out the changes in the public life of the empire, from A.D. 200 to 400, and then retrace my steps to analyze those less public, but equally decisive, changes in religious attitudes that took place over the same period. I have done my best to indicate where I consider that changes in the social and economic conditions of the empire intermingled with the religious developments of the age.

Throughout this period, the Mediterranean and Mesopotamia are the main theaters of change. The world of the northern barbarians remained peripheral to these areas. Britain, northern Gaul, the Danubian provinces after the Slav invasions of the late sixth century fall outside my purview. The narrative itself gravitates towards the eastern Mediterranean; the account ends more naturally at the Baghdad of Harun al-Rashid than at the remote Aachen of his contemporary,

Charlemagne. I trust that the reader (and especially the medievalist who is accustomed to surveys that concentrate on the emergence of a post-Roman western society) will forgive me if I keep to this area. For western Europe, he will have those sure guides, to whom we are both equally indebted.

No one can deny the close links between the social and the spiritual revolution of the Late Antique period. Yet, just because they are so intimate, such links cannot be reduced to a superficial relationship of "cause and effect." Often, the historian can only say that certain changes coincided in such a way that the one cannot be understood without reference to the other. A history of the Late Antique world that is all emperors and barbarians, soldiers, landlords and tax-collectors would give as colorless and as unreal a picture of the quality of the age, as would an account devoted only to the sheltered souls, to the monks, the mystics, and the awesome theologians of that time. I must leave it to the reader to decide whether my account helps him to understand why so many changes, of such different kinds, converged to produce that very distinctive period of European civilization — the Late Antique world.

The Boundaries of the Classical World: c. A.D. 200

"We live round a sea," Socrates had told his Athenian friends, "like frogs round a pond." Seven hundred years later, in A.D. 200, the classical world remained clustered round its "pond": it still clung to the shores of the Mediterranean. The centers of modern Europe lie far to the north and to the west of the world of ancient men. To travel to the Rhineland, for them, was to go "half-way to the barbarians": one typical southerner even took his dead wife all the way back home, from Trier to Pavia, to bury her safely with her ancestors! A Greek senator from Asia Minor, posted to a governorship on the Danube, could only pity himself: "The inhabitants . . . lead the most miserable existence of all mankind," he wrote, "for they cultivate no olives and they drink no wine."

The Roman Empire had been extended as far as had seemed necessary at the time of the republic and the early empire, to protect and enrich the classical world that had already existed for centuries round the coast of the Mediterranean. It is the extraordinary tide of Mediterranean life that strikes us about this empire at its apogee in the second century A.D. This tide had washed further inland than ever previously; in North Africa and the Near East, it would never reach as far again. For a short time, an officers' mess modeled on an Italian country-villa faced the Grampians in Scotland. A checkerboard town, with amphitheater, library and statues of classical philosophers looked out over the Hodna range, at Timgad, in what are now the bleak southern territories of Algeria. At Dura-Europos, on the Euphrates, a garrison-town observed the same calendar of public festivals as at Rome. The Late Antique world inherited this amazing legacy. One of the main problems of the period from 200 to 700 was how to maintain, throughout a vast empire, a style of life and a culture based originally on a slender coastline studded with classical city-states.

In the first place, the classical Mediterranean had always been a world on the edge of starvation. For the Mediterranean is a sea surrounded by mountain ranges: its fertile plains and river-valleys are like pieces of lace sewn on to sackcloth. Many of the greatest cities of classical times were placed within sight of forbidding highlands. Every year their inhabitants ransacked the surrounding countryside to feed themselves. Describing the symptoms of widespread malnutrition in the countryside in the middle of the second century, the doctor Galen observed:

> *The city-dwellers, as was their practice, collected and stored enough corn for all the coming year immediately after the harvest. They carried off all the wheat, the barley, the beans and the lentils and left what remained to the countryfolk.*

Seen in this light, the history of the Roman Empire is the history of the ways in which 10 percent of the population, who lived in the towns and have left their mark on the course of European civilization, fed themselves, in the summary manner described by Galen, from the labors of the remaining 90 percent who worked the land.

Food was the most precious commodity in the ancient Mediterranean. Food involved transport. Very few of the great cities of the Roman Empire could hope to supply their own needs from their immediate environment. Rome had long depended on the annual sailing of the grain-fleet from Africa: by the sixth century A.D., Constantinople drew 175,200 tons of wheat a year from Egypt.

Water is to all primitive systems of transport what railways have been in modern times: the one, indispensable artery for heavy freight. Once a cargo left the waters of the Mediterranean or of a great river, its brisk and inexpensive progress changed to a ruinous slow-motion. It cost less to bring a cargo of grain from one end of the Mediterranean to another than to carry it another seventy-five miles inland.

So the Roman Empire always consisted of two, overlapping worlds. Up to A.D. 700, great towns by the sea remained close to each other: twenty days of clear sailing would take the traveler from one end of the Mediterranean, the core of the Roman world, to the other. Inland, however, Roman life had always tended to coagulate in little oases, like drops of water on a drying surface. The Romans are renowned for the roads that ran through their empire: but the roads passed through towns where the inhabitants gained all that they ate, and most of what they used, from within a radius of only thirty miles.

It was inland, therefore, that the heavy cost of empire was most obvious, along the verges of the great land routes. The Roman Empire appears at its most cumbersome and brutal in the ceaseless effort it made to hold itself together. Soldiers, administrators, couriers, their supplies, had to be constantly on the move from province to province. Seen by the emperors in 200, the Roman world had become a cobweb of roads, marked by the staging-posts at which each little community would have to assemble ever-increasing levies of food, clothing, animals and manpower to support the court and the army.

As for those who served the needs of this rough machine, such compulsions were, at least, nothing new. In places, they were as old as civilization itself. In Palestine, for instance, Christ had warned his hearers how to behave when an official should "requisition you to walk with him (carrying his baggage) for a mile." Even the word the Evangelist used for "requisition" was not, originally, a Greek word: it derived from the Persian, it dated back over five hundred years, to the days when the Achaemenids had stocked the famous roads of their vast empire by the same rough methods.

Yet the Roman Empire, that had sprawled so dangerously far from the Mediterranean by 200, was held together by the illusion that it was still a very small world. Seldom has a state been so dependent on so delicate a sleight of hand. By 200, the empire was ruled by an aristocracy of amazingly uniform culture, taste and language. In the West, the senatorial class had remained a tenacious and absorptive elite that dominated Italy, Africa, the Midi of France and the valleys of the Ebro and the Guadalquivir; in the East, all culture and all local power had remained concentrated in the hands of the proud oligarchies of the Greek cities. Throughout the Greek world no difference in vocabulary or pronunciation would betray the birthplace of any well-educated speaker. In the West, bilingual aristocrats passed unself-consciously from Latin to Greek; an African landowner, for instance, found himself quite at home in a literary *salon* of well-to-do Greeks at Smyrna.

Such astonishing uniformity, however, was maintained by men who felt obscurely that their classical culture existed to exclude alternatives to their own world. Like many cosmopolitan aristocracies — like the dynasts of late feudal Europe or the aristocrats of the Austro-Hungarian Empire — men of the same class and culture, in any part of the Roman world, found themselves far closer to each other than to the vast majority of their neighbors, the "underdeveloped" peasantry on their doorstep. The existence of the "barbarian" exerted a silent, unremitting pressure on the culture of the Roman Empire. The "barbarian" was not only the primitive warrior from across the frontier: by 200, this "barbarian" had been joined by the nonparticipant within the empire itself. The aristocrat would pass from reassuringly similar forum to forum, speaking a uniform language, observing rites and codes of behavior shared by all educated men; but his road stretched through the territories of tribesmen that were as alien to him as any German or Persian. In Gaul, the countrymen still spoke Celtic; in North Africa, Punic and Libyan; in Asia Minor, ancient dialects such as Lycaonian, Phrygian and Cappadocian; in Syria, Aramaic and Syriac.

Living cheek by jowl with this immense unabsorbed "barbarian" world, the governing classes of the Roman Empire had kept largely free of some of the more virulent exclusiveness of modern colonial regimes: they were notoriously tolerant of race and of local religions. But the price they demanded for inclusion in their own world was conformity — the adoption of its style of life, of its traditions, of its education, and so of its two classical languages, Latin in the West and Greek in the East. Those who were in no position to participate were dismissed: they were frankly despised as "country-bumpkins" and "barbarians." Those who could have participated and did not — most notably the Jews — were treated with varying degrees of hatred and contempt, only occasionally tempered by respectful curiosity for the representatives of an ancient Near Eastern civilization. Those who had once participated and had ostentatiously "dropped out" — namely the Christians — were liable to summary execution. By A.D. 200 many provincial governors and many mobs had had occasion to assert the boundaries of the classical world with hysterical certainty against the Christian dissenter in their midst: as one magistrate told Christians, "I cannot bring myself so much as to listen to people who speak ill of the Roman way of religion."

Classical society of about A.D. 200 was a society with firm boundaries. Yet it was far from being a stagnant society. In the Greek world, the classical tradition had already existed for some seven hundred years. Its first burst of creativity, at Athens, should not blind us to the astonishing way in which, from the time of the conquests of Alexander the Great, Greek culture had settled down to a rhythm of survival — as drawn-out, as capable of exquisite nuance, as patient of repetition as a plain-chant. One exciting renaissance had taken place in the second century A.D. It coincided with a revival of the economic life and the political initiative of the upper classes of the Greek cities. The age of the Antonines was the heyday of the Greek Sophists. These men — known for their devotion to rhetoric — were at one and the same time literary lions and great urban nabobs. They enjoyed vast influence and popularity: one of them, Polemo of Smyrna, "treated whole cities as his inferiors, emperors as not his superiors and gods . . . as equals." Behind them stood the thriving cities of the Aegean. The huge classical remains at Ephesus and Smyrna (and, indeed, similar contemporary cities and temples, from Lepcis Magna in Tunisia to Baalbek in the Lebanon) seem to us nowadays to sum up a timeless ancient world. They were, in fact, the creation of only a few generations of baroque magnificence, between Hadrian (117–138) and Septimius Severus (193–211).

It is just at the end of the second and the beginning of the third centuries, also, that the Greek culture was garnered which formed the ballast of the classical tradition throughout the Middle Ages. The encyclopedias, the handbooks of medicine, natural science and astronomy, to which all cultivated men — Latins, Byzantines, Arabs — turned for the next fifteen hundred years, were compiled then. Literary tastes and political attitudes that continued, in the Greek world, until the end of the Middle Ages, were first formed in the age of the Antonines: Byzantine gentlemen of the fifteenth century were still using a recondite Attic Greek deployed by the Sophists of the age of Hadrian.

At this time the Greek world made the Roman Empire its own. We can appreciate this identification with the Roman state and the subtle shifts of emphasis it entailed, by looking at a Greek from Bithynia, who had joined the Roman governing class as a senator — Dio Cassius, who wrote his *Roman History* up to A.D. 229. No matter how enthusiastically Dio had absorbed the outlook of the Roman Senate, we are constantly reminded that the empire had come to Greeks accustomed to centuries of enlightened despotism. Dio knew that the Roman emperor was an autocrat. Common decency and a shared interest with the educated upper classes were the only checks on his behavior — not the delicate clockwork of the constitution of Augustus. And Dio knew how fragile such restraints could be: he had been present at a meeting of the Senate when an astrologer had denounced certain "bald-pated men" for conspiring against the emperor . . . instinctively his hand had shot up to feel the top of his head. But Dio accepted the strong rule of one man as long as it gave him an orderly world: only the emperor could suppress civil war; only he could police the faction-ridden Greek cities; only he could make Dio's class secure and respected. Byzantine scholars who turned to Dio, centuries later, to know about Roman history, found themselves hopelessly at sea in his account of the heroes of the Roman republic: but they were able to understand perfectly the strong and conscientious emperors of Dio's own age — already the Roman history of a Greek of the late second and early third century A.D. was *their* history.

A shift of the center of gravity of the Roman Empire towards the Greek cities of Asia Minor, a flowering of a Greek mandarinate — in these ways, the palmy days of the Antonines already point in the direction of Byzantium. But the men of the age of Dio Cassius still resolutely faced the other way: they were stalwart conservatives; their greatest successes had been expressed in a cultural reaction; for them, the boundaries of the classical world were still clear and rigid — Byzantium proper, a civilization that could build, on top of this ancient backward-looking tradition, such revolutionary novelties as the establishment of Christianity and the foundation of Constantinople as a "New Rome," was inconceivable to a man like Dio. (He never, for instance, so much as mentions the existence of Christianity, although Christians had worried the authorities in his home-country for over 150 years.) Such a civilization could only emerge in the late Roman revolution of the third and fourth centuries A.D.

* * *

The theme that will emerge throughout this book is the shifting and redefinition of the boundaries of the classical world after A.D. 200. This has little to do with the conventional problem of the "Decline and Fall of the Roman Empire." The "Decline and Fall" affected only the political structure of the western provinces of the Roman Empire: it left the cultural powerhouse of Late Antiquity — the eastern Mediterranean and the Near East — unscathed. Even in the barbarian states of western Europe, in the sixth and seventh centuries, the Roman Empire, as it survived at Constantinople, was still regarded as the greatest civilized state in the world: and it was called by its ancient name, the *Respublica*. The problem that urgently preoccupied men of Late Antiquity themselves was, rather, the painful modification of the ancient boundaries.

Geographically, the hold of the Mediterranean slackened. After 410 Britain was abandoned; after 480 Gaul came to be firmly ruled from the north. In the East, paradoxically, the rolling back of the Mediterranean had happened earlier and more imperceptibly; but it proved decisive. Up to the first century A.D., a veneer of Greek civilization still covered large areas of the Iranian plateau: a Greco-Buddhist art had flourished in Afghanistan, and the decrees of a Buddhist ruler have been found outside Kabul, translated into impeccable philosophical Greek. In 224, however, a family from Fars, the "Deep South" of Iranian chauvinism, gained control of the Persian Empire. The revived Persian Empire of this, the Sassanian, dynasty quickly shook the Greek fancy-dress from its shoulders. An efficient and aggressive empire, whose ruling classes were notably unreceptive to western influence, now stood on the eastern frontiers of the Roman Empire. In 252, 257 and again in 260, the great Shahanshah, the king of kings, Shapur I, showed what terrible damage his mailed horsemen could do:

> *Valerian the Caesar came against us with seventy thousand men . . . and we fought a great battle against him, and we took Valerian the*

Caesar with our own hands. . . . And the provinces of Syria, Cilicia and Cappadocia we burnt with fire, we ravaged and conquered them, taking their peoples captive.

The fear of repeating such an experience tilted the balance of the emperor's concern further from the Rhine and ever nearer to the Euphrates. What is more, the confrontation with Sassanian Persia breached the barriers of the classical world in the Near East: for it gave prominence to Mesopotamia, and so exposed the Roman world to constant influence from that area of immense, exotic creativity in art and religion.

It is not always the conventional dates that are the most decisive. Everyone knows that the Goths sacked Rome in 410: but the lost western provinces of the empire remained a recognizably "sub-Roman" civilization for centuries. By contrast, when the eastern provinces of the empire were lost to Islam after 640, these did not long remain "sub-Byzantine" societies: they were rapidly "orientalized." For Islam itself was pulled far to the east of its original conquests by the vast mass of the conquered Persian Empire. In the eighth century the Mediterranean seaboard came to be ruled from Baghdad; the Mediterranean became a backwater to men who were used to sailing from the Persian Gulf; and the court of Harun al-Rashid (788–809), with its heavy trappings of "sub-Persian" culture, was a reminder that the irreversible victory of the Near East over the Greeks began slowly but surely with the revolt of Fars in A.D. 224.

As the Mediterranean receded, so a more ancient world came to light. Craftsmen in Britain returned to the art forms of the La Tène age. The serf of late Roman Gaul reemerged with his Celtic name — the *vassus*. The arbiters of piety of the Roman world, the Coptic hermits of Egypt, revived the language of the Pharaohs; and the hymn-writers of Syria heaped on Christ appellations of Divine Kingship that reach back to Sumerian times. Round the Mediterranean itself, inner barriers collapsed. Another side of the Roman world, often long prepared in obscurity, came to the top, like different-colored loam turned by the plow. Three generations after Dio Cassius had ignored it, Christianity became the religion of the emperors. Small things sometimes betray changes more faithfully, because unconsciously. Near Rome, a sculptor's yard of the fourth century still turned out statues, impeccably dressed in the old Roman toga (with a socket for detachable portrait-heads!); but the aristocrats who commissioned such works would, in fact, wear a costume which betrayed prolonged exposure to the "barbarians" of the non-Mediterranean world — a woollen shirt from the Danube, a cloak from northern Gaul, fastened at the shoulders by a filigree brooch from Germany, even guarding their health by "Saxon" trousers. Deeper still, at the very core of the Mediterranean, the tradition of Greek philosophy had found a way of opening itself to a different religious mood.

Such changes as these are the main themes of the evolution of the Late Antique world.

Ramsay MacMullen

Social Transformation

The purpose of this book is to show how energies both harmonious and hostile to the Roman order appeared in a given class at a given time. As the locus of these energies moved down the social scale in the course of the first four centuries of the Empire, so the enemies of the state were, to begin with, drawn from senatorial ranks and, in the end, from peasants and barbarians. The drift of directing power outward and downward from the Roman aristocracy is well known; its corollary is the simultaneous movement of anti-Establishment impulses in the same direction. I can see no significant struggle of slave against free or poor against rich. Protest originated within whatever classes were dominant at different periods. Perhaps that is what we should expect. The French Revolution, favorite cadaver for historical dissection, offers all the signs of a narrowly internal disease, the bourgeois fomenting reforms of a system they themselves controlled. The phenomenon is typical. History, as it is not one of the semiexact, or social, sciences, does not easily accommodate theories; people, *deo gratias*, retain the right to be puzzling; but the patterns detected here seem to fit times and peoples other than Roman.

At any rate, when the story of the empire begins, it is men like Brutus who crowd the councils of the monarch, and who murder monarchy, as they think, on the Ides of March. Had Caesar been able to tell friends from foes, he would have survived that day, but they appeared identical down to the smallest detail of family and origin, of earlier careers and training, of accent and dress, of enthusiasm for a good prose style that Caesar ardently shared. A century later the descendants of this group of pro- and anti-Caesarians, somewhat mixed now with a newer nobility, were still supplying both supporters and destroyers of the throne, the two so similar that in fact many members of one allegiance — Seneca or Lucan, let us say — passed over to the other without giving up any essential belief. There have always been men who switched sides, of course; they have often insisted that it was rather the rest of the world that changed, not themselves; still, it is striking how interchangeable and ambiguous were the attitudes of the different groups in the aristocracy, how Janus-faced they were, looking toward the past, *libertas*, and senate, and at the same time toward the future, stability, and the emperor. The emperor himself often cultivated the literature that nerved his subjects to speak out, the astrology that they pursued at the risk of capital punishment, and the rhetorical exercises that extolled tyrannicide. Literature, astrology, and rhetoric, like their practitioners, were sources of possible danger to the throne. They were also characteristic to the Roman establishment. Add the old families, political marriages, and Stoicism. The operation of these latter factors, too, in the circles of the emperor's enemies, is obvious.

In sources for the history of the opposition in the first century, that is, in Tacitus above all, and Seneca, and Pliny, the dominant figures are men of high birth whose home is Italy. The making of events belongs to them even if their dearest ambition sometimes seems to be the unmaking of events and the return to an age long past, whether Cato's or Zeno's or Aristogeiton's. Succeeding generations admitted an increasing admixture of recruits to the inner circle of influence. Tacitus's family may have come from southern Gaul, Seneca's was Spanish. In the second century the very emperors were no longer exclusively Italian. Their friends — Herodes Atticus, Avidius Cassius — might be Greek or Syrian. Opening opportunities for colonials by no means guaranteed their loyalty. Herodes participated in a movement, the so-called Second Sophistic, perfectly harmless on the surface but anti-Roman in its implications, since its intent was the reassertion of Hellenism. As for Avidius Cassius, he rebelled, getting help from his countrymen. For a time thereafter an attempt was made to assign officers to provinces other than those of their birth. Events proved the precaution pointless and it was abandoned. The list of revolts and pretenders over the next two hundred years reveals no pattern of "Syria for the Syrians" or of aid given only to native sons. Not separatism but power without definition found expression as much in Herodes Atticus as in Cassius; for the first benefit of power has always been to use it as one pleases. Once a share had passed from the more generous or slackening grasp of Tacitus's like to a wider circle, it was destined to appear embodied in a thousand shapes, some harmonious with the historic aims and character of Rome, some otherwise. The provincial elite under the Antonines played on a far wider stage the same ambiguous role as the older Roman elite had played in the capital a century earlier.

Developments that gave a chance to leaders in the provinces to assert themselves worked equally in favor of once-despised classes in Italy as everywhere else. They attained wealth and influence without wholly abandoning their inheritance. A love of gaudily colored clothes, for example, slowly grew upon the upper classes, though much of the style seems to have originated among circus habitués. In the Greek East, plebeian enthusiasms for gladiation in the end infected the aristocracy. As medical science stagnated, a scum of superstition rose to the surface: the gods could reveal cures in dreams, hence the crowds of consulars thronging the shrines of Asclepius as never before, to talk to him, and no doubt ceaselessly to each other, about their stomach disorders and arthritic joints. The number and artistry of amulets rises in the third and fourth centuries. St. Basil assumes their popularity in his congregation. "Is your boy sick? Then you search out the incantation expert, or someone who will put a charm with curious characters on it around the necks of innocent children" — such a charm, perhaps, as the encyclopedic authority of Alexander of Tralles recommended for colic, to be worn as a necklace or a ring; while at the other extremity of the empire, a Gallic peasant who got something stuck in his throat invoked his ancestral gods in Celtic in a spell duly recorded by medical handbooks: "Rub out of the throat, out of the gullet, Aisus, remove thou thyself my evil out of the throat, out of the gorge."

Testimony here to the rise of popular culture into the ruling classes;

testimony also to the tenacious conservatism characterizing beliefs in the supernatural. As Celtic, a language living only among the poor and the isolated, found its way into books in the form of an incantation, so the last inscriptions in Phrygian, of the third century, are predominantly curse formulas; and of a similar nature, by the third century, the development of a usable alphabet for the Egyptian tongue answered the needs of religion and its literature embodied in various hagiologies and Last Judgment scenes a great deal of the fellahin's immemorial dreads, visions, and symbols. Archeologists working with a totally different kind of evidence report parallel findings. The dominant culture of the empire exerted its strongest influence on the material plane, while unmaterial aspects such as cults and superstitions remained least affected. If Romanization worked least on the unmaterial plane, it follows that an un-Roman religion, Christianity, attaining riches and power, could elevate with it to official favor the beliefs and tastes that had laid hitherto hidden away among the masses. That conclusion can in fact be confirmed through the study of such scattered subjects as late antique art, literary metaphors, and ideas of social justice.

The life that Tacitus knew because he saw it among the tenant farmers who worked his fields, or among the troops that he must surely have commanded at some time in his career, had its own force of growth needing only the stimulation of opportunity to express itself through its risen heroes: peasants chosen as abbots, freedman become municipal councilors, the sons of barbarian irregulars clothed with high government office by that loosening of society typical of the third century and still effective in the fourth. Tacitus, however, would have insisted that Roman civilization meant something higher and narrower: the capital; more, the great within it; eloquence and philology; the Ara Pacis and the Temple of Concord. It was from this world that rules reached down to give structure to the life of the masses.

With consensus very flattering to Tacitus's smugness, modern assessments of what Rome achieved emphasize much the same things; but the distortion here is evident. What is outstanding is by definition untypical; what rules forbid does not cease to exist. No doubt illegal resorts to magic were more important to the bulk of the population than visits to publicly acknowledged divinities, even though less obvious in our sources. Relative lack of evidence proves nothing. Consider, by way of analogy, how much of today's literature and how rich a selection of material remains might be known without ever hinting at the modern popularity of gambling. Equally true of many private associations, lacking even a name, simply friends and neighbors meeting every Monday afternoon, now as then hardly the concern of historians. Inhabitants of the Roman Empire were continually forming clubs of every conceivable description, despite laws that might, for all their elasticity, be at any moment invoked against them. And again, despite legislation that forbade slander or treasonous publications, the ordinary citizen told his rulers what he thought of them in furtive doggerel posted on statues or, safe in a crowd, in rhythmic shouts at the theater. This was democracy, of a sort; clubs demonstrated sociability; and superstition demonstrated religiosity — all three, aspects of popular culture, and not a whit less Roman for being actually illegal. In the later Empire, all three were admitted to a public role. Membership in associations was positively enforced; whole cities bought amulets to ward off plagues and earthquakes; and leaders of Church and state had their cause noised abroad in polemical songs or in the unison chanting of some theatrical or senatorial audience: "'Claudius Augustus, may the gods preserve you,' said sixty times; 'Claudius Augustus, you or your like we have always desired as emperor,' said forty times."

Rostovtzeff ended his incomparable *Social and Economic History of the Roman Empire* with two famous questions: "Is it possible to extend a higher civilization to the lower classes without debasing its standard and diluting its quality to the vanishing point? Is not every civilization bound to decay as soon as it begins to penetrate the masses?" The assumption behind his despair is Tacitean: there is one drop of purple — let us take that, the color of the senatorial stripe and, for Epictetus, the blazon of moral eminence — one drop of purple in a pool of water. Dilution destroys it. But, as Rostovtzeff showed better than anyone else has done, civilization is the whole pool, and all its levels possess a distinctive color. Pursuits of the lower classes forbidden by the nobility or excluded by them from what they would have defined as Roman nevertheless had their own vital principle. The unlawful and un-Roman can be kept out of history only if it is written by people of the purple stripe.

Illyricum supplies a final illustration of what I am getting at. Here (less clearly than in the Rhine provinces, to be sure) archeologists have discovered traces of decorative arts driven off the field by the competition of classicizing tastes in the first and earlier second centuries, reclaiming a part of their popularity in the late second, third, and fourth centuries, and joining other local customs and beliefs which had never been much changed to form a cultural whole. This latter was certainly un-Roman, though not in any aggressive sense of the term. Yet the same area and the same population produced the savior dynasties of the later Empire. They appeared before the middle of the third century, tightened their grip on power right through the fourth century, and over that long, long duration of crisis succeeded in keeping far more hostile and un-Roman forces than themselves at bay. Was Illyricum un-Roman, then? No more than the senate of the first century, from which came the enemies of the state as well as its chief upholders. What had occurred in the interval was a shift in the locus of energy. Its causes do not concern us here. Its effects are detectable in the increasing prominence of actors barely participant in the drama of the earlier Empire, gradually coming forward to the center of the stage. Sometimes they appeared as aberrant or destructive to the civilization in which they originated; they have then supplied the chief focus for this book [*Enemies of the Roman Order*]; at other times they spoke, as it were, for the majority; but in either case, the broad lines of Roman and un-Roman history trace the same course.

Arther Ferrill

The Empire Fell

Perhaps the most popular approach to the period in the last generation has been to deny the fall altogether — to emphasize the continuity between Rome and the Middle Ages. Peter Brown in his book, *The World of Late Antiquity, A.D. 150–750* (1971), generally ignores the fall and the barbarians (or at least the implications of the word, "barbarians"). He concentrates instead on the transformation from Roman to Byzantine history in the East and to a certain extent from Roman to early medieval history in the West. On the whole the emphasis of the "Late Antique" school is positive and up-beat — it is on change rather than collapse and cataclysm, on spirituality in religion rather than

From *The Fall of the Roman Empire: A Military Explanation* by Arther Ferrill, 1986. Reprinted by permission of Thames and Hudson Ltd., London.

superstition. "Savage barbarians" and "Germanity" have little role to play in the world of "Late Antiquity," and Brown's approach has attracted many followers.

It is not difficult to understand the ennui now felt by historians confronted with the fall of Rome. There is a feeling of hopelessness, that no one will ever find an answer that will satisfy the majority of scholars. Nor has there been any significant "new evidence" since Gibbon's day. There have been relatively few important literary discoveries, and, although some interesting archaeological work on the Late Empire has been undertaken, archaeologists generally are more attracted to the romantic fields of Egypt and Mesopotamia, the Minoan and Mycenaean world, and Periclean Athens.

Another reason for discontent with the "problem" of Rome's fall is that many of the best-known explanations, even in some instances those offered by otherwise outstanding ancient historians, are frivolous or absurd. Michael Rostovtzeff's monumental, two-volume *Social and Economic History of the Roman Empire* (originally published in 1926) deserves for many reasons the high repute it has enjoyed, but Rostovtzeff's explanation of the fall of Rome — a class struggle in which the army became involved on the side of the peasants — is nonsense. So too is Tenney Frank's view that race mixture, or the debilitating influence of the East on the West, caused the fall of Rome, although Frank was in other respects one of the greatest Roman historians in the first half of the twentieth century.

Then there are the "seed" or "germ" theories which trace the reasons for the fall of Rome so far back into the period of Roman greatness that they become remote from the events of the fourth and fifth centuries (the "Downhill-all-the-way" school). Gibbon began with the Antonines and regretted after he finished his work that he had not begun even earlier. Apparently simple explanations, usually variations of the "Downhill-all-the-way" approach, such as climatic changes, the decline of population, and lead poisoning have had some popular appeal but few adherents among professional historians.

Likewise some historians are undoubtedly troubled by the polemical or "topical" nature of attempts at explanation: "reflecting the problems of those who propounded them," wrote F. W. Walbank, "and designed to illuminate what was dark in contemporary life." In the fifth century Christians blamed the pagans and pagans blamed the

Christians. In the twentieth century writers concerned with growing bureaucracy or immorality in modern life commonly see bureaucracy or immorality as the cause of Rome's fall. The obvious absurdity of some of the arguments seems to make little difference. Morality, in the Christian sense in which the word is normally intended, was much greater in the fourth and fifth centuries than it had been before. If immorality contributed to Rome's fall, why did it take so long?

The main line of substantial scholarly research into the fall of Rome, however, particularly in England but elsewhere as well, has emphasized that the fall of the Western Empire in the fifth century was a cataclysmic event, a sharp break in European history, and that the invasion of the barbarians was the chief act in the story. In the last two hundred years, three works in particular stand out: Gibbon's *Decline and Fall*, J. B. Bury's two-volume *History of the Later Roman Empire*, 395–565 (1923), and A. H. M. Jones' multi-volume *The Later Roman Empire*, 294–602 (1964). All three emphasize the role played by the barbarians in the fall of Rome. Even in languages other than English, that view has been a significant one. One of the most respected accounts of the Late Empire in French, Andre Piganiol's *L'Empire Chrétien* (325–395) (2nd ed., 1972) concludes:

> *It is too easy to say that upon the arrival of the barbarians in the empire "everything was dead, it was a powerless corpse, a body stretched out in its own blood," or that the Roman Empire in the West was not destroyed by a brutal blow, but that it was "sleeping."*
>
> *Roman civilization did not die a natural death. It was killed.*

In German scholarship the age of the barbarian invasions, the so-called *Völkerwanderung*, has understandably attracted somewhat more attention, and there is a kind of nationalistic bias in favour of change rather than continuity. The idea that "Germanity" combined with Christianity to add a strikingly new dimension to Graeco-Roman classical civilization has naturally had a strong appeal and indeed has influenced scholars outside Germany.

In many ways A. H. M. Jones' panoramic treatment of the fall of Rome is most representative of the mainline tradition. One of his greatest contributions to the problem was an important and obviously correct distinction — the Roman Empire did not fall in the fifth century: it continued to survive in the East in what we know as the Byzantine

Empire until the Turkish conquest in the middle of the fifteenth century. Therefore, when we speak of the fall of Rome, a perfectly legitimate expression as long as everyone understands exactly what is meant by it, we refer only to the western half of the Roman Empire, and any explanation of the fall of the West must take into account the survival of the East.

"These facts are important," Jones wrote, "for they demonstrate that the empire did not, as some modern historians have suggested, totter into its grave from senile decay, impelled by a gentle push from the barbarians. Most of the internal weaknesses which these historians stress were common to both halves of the empire." If Christianity weakened the Empire internally, since the religion was stronger and more divisive in the East, why did the West fall and the East continue to stand? The evils of bureaucracy, of social rigidity, of the economic system, were all present in the East as well as the West.

The main difference, as Jones accurately saw it, was that "down to the end of the fifth century" the East was "strategically less vulnerable" and "subjected to less pressure from external enemies." In short, the barbarian invasion of the West was the main cause of the fall of Rome. The Western emperors of the fifth century could not stop attacks from both the Rhine and the Danube whereas the Eastern emperor more easily held Constantinople, a superbly fortified capital. Trouble with Persia threatened the East, but Romans for various reasons found the Persians easier to deal with than the barbarians. For one thing Persians were not migratory. They had their own internal problems, and they could be dealt with according to the well developed protocol of ancient diplomacy.

In a somewhat less persuasive section Jones dismisses civil war and rebellion as major causes of the decline and fall because the fourth and fifth centuries saw less of them than the earlier period of imperial history. That is debatable, and so is Jones' view that the Roman army had not been neglected and that in certain respects it was superior to the more famous army of the Early Empire. It was larger, and it had more cavalry, but whether after Constantine it pursued a "wiser strategy" in abandoning preclusive security along the frontiers is much less certain than Jones believed. On the whole his survey of the "fighting quality" of the late imperial army was too optimistic. The frontier garrisons were inferior to the central reserve and "barbarization" of the Roman army was a serious problem, not, as Jones saw it, a source of strength. When he wrote that "No career officer of German origin . . . is ever known to have betrayed the interests of the empire to his countrymen," he may have been correct, but the loyalty of barbarian officers is not really the issue, as we shall see.

On the other hand, Jones correctly argued that the decay of trade and industry was not a cause of Rome's fall. There was a decline in agriculture and land was withdrawn from cultivation, in some cases on a very large scale, sometimes as a direct result of barbarian invasions. However, the chief cause of the agricultural decline was high taxation on marginal land, driving it out of cultivation. Jones is surely right in saying that taxation was spurred by the huge military budget and was thus "indirectly" the result of the barbarian invasions.

The evidence for another often mentioned problem, depopulation, is not very strong. The existing statistics are notoriously unreliable, and not many figures are available anyway, but population probably did decline. After reviewing the evidence Jones concludes that the city of Rome had a population of 500,000 to 750,000 around A.D. 300 (down from perhaps 1,000,000 at the death of Augustus in A.D. 14); that Constantinople was the same size by the sixth century; and that Alexandria in the sixth century was half as large as Constantinople. Antioch may have had somewhere between 150,000 and 200,000 inhabitants. On the whole Jones sees "no significant difference" between the birth and death rates of the Early and Late Empire (both of which were high).

Strangely, there is much evidence for manpower shortages, as opposed to depopulation, in the Late Empire. That is why workers were bound to their occupations under Diocletian, Constantine and their successors, and it is why tenants (*coloni*) were tied to the soil. Plague and famine, compounded by the disruptions of the barbarian invasions, also took their toll. After paying rent and taxes the peasants of the Empire simply could not afford to support all their children at a subsistence level. Infanticide and malnutrition had their effect, on the urban poor as well as the peasantry, and the population shrank, but, according to Jones, "it was not in most areas catastrophic." The increasing demands of the church, the governmental bureaucracy, and the army, however, exacerbated the manpower shortage. Yet no matter what the number of people in the Roman Empire, it was certainly much greater than the barbarians who invaded.

One result of the decline of population was that the number of producers sank while the number of "idle mouths" stayed the same or possibly increased (particularly with the demands on manpower created by the increases in military forces). Social regimentation more or less guaranteed that there would be idle mouths to feed, since regimentation puts people firmly at the top of society as well as at the bottom. On the other hand, the rigidity of the law tying Romans to their occupations was accompanied by a laxity in enforcement, and there were many escape valves. The frequency of such laws in the Late Empire reminds one of the laws against bribery and corruption in the days of Caesar and suggests that in this case it was easier to legislate than to police. It is also true that many more commoners rose to high position in the Late Empire than in the days of Augustus.

Although corruption in government was a greater problem in the Late Empire than it had been earlier, partly because the civil bureaucracy had grown larger, Jones argues convincingly that relative to the size of the Empire the number of governmental officials (which he estimates at about thirty thousand) was not great and that this expense was small. More significant than corruption as a sign of the times was what Jones called the "absence of public spirit" or the "decline of morale." Pride in the Empire and in the cities certainly diminished, and the lack of public spirit showed itself in the passive manner in which Romans in the West faced the barbarian invasions. There are some notable exceptions, of course, but Romans generally seem simply to have fled when they did not meekly submit. The apathy and docility of the Roman population need not reflect a grave societal malaise; for centuries unarmed Romans had relied on the protection of a great professional army.

Finally Jones notes that there were two ways in which the East was stronger than the West. The East was "richer and more populous," and wealth was more evenly distributed; there were more peasants, more "medium landowners" and fewer aristocrats. In the West the aristocracy was incredibly wealthy, and it was more influential in its region of the Empire than the eastern aristocracy was with the emperor in Constantinople, where imperial autocracy reigned. Because the economic resources were greater in the East, governmental revenues were less limited. In the fifth century emperors at Constantinople paid enormous sums in bribes to the barbarians to go west, whereas western rulers faced crushing fiscal burdens.

In the end, however, according to Jones, the "major cause" of the fall of Rome in the West was that the West "was more exposed to barbarian onslaughts." The concluding sentence of his massive study of the Late Roman Empire reads: "The internal weaknesses of the empire cannot have been a major factor in its decline." This view carries respected authority; it was in fact the internal structure of the Roman Empire that Jones knew best. One of the ironies of his work is that in a multi-volume book dealing in intricate detail with the internal social, economic and administrative structure of the Empire, the author argued that external pressure caused its fall.

Naturally, we need not slavishly follow Jones' views. He was often more circumspect in stating them than the paraphrase above might suggest. Furthermore, he was not invariably correct; for example, his assessment of the Roman army in the fourth and fifth centuries requires significant modification. But, on the whole, the emphasis on barbarian pressures rather than on internal weakness is surely justified, and his careful analysis of all the symptoms of decay highlighted by other historians is generally persuasive.

Jones' arguments, of course, do not dispose of the advocates of continuity, as opposed to change, in the transformation from the Roman Empire to the Middle Ages. Peter Brown and the "Late Antique" school (along with those historians who see in the West the perpetuation of Roman economic, social, administrative and legal patterns into the sixth and seventh centuries) generally deny the reality of the cataclysmic fall of Rome. The fact is, however, that the two points of view are not necessarily contradictory, and their adherents need not clash as much as they seem to.

It is quite possible that many significant features of Roman life survived the overthrow of the last emperor in the West, Romulus Augustulus, in 476. Obviously they did in the East, and in the West too one would expect to see major Roman survivals in the economy, in society and in law. The advocates of change are much too strident in their insistence that the fall of Rome destroyed everything Roman. Likewise, the advocates of continuity all too often ignore the obvious fact that not everything survived the barbarian invasions of the fifth century, that indeed dramatically significant changes occurred in the West from A.D. 400 to 500.

In fact the Roman Empire of the West did fall. Not every aspect of the life of Roman subjects was changed by that, but the fall of Rome as a political entity was one of the major events of the history of western man. It will simply not do to call that fall a myth or to ignore its historical significance merely by focussing on those aspects of Roman life that survived the fall in one form or another. At the opening of the fifth century a massive army, perhaps more than 200,000 strong, stood at the service of the Western emperor and his generals. In 476 it was gone. The destruction of Roman military power in the fifth century A.D. was the obvious cause of the collapse of Roman government in the West.

Suggestions for Additional Reading

The best introduction to the problem remains Edward Gibbon's *Decline and Fall of the Roman Empire*, in the J. B. Bury edition (7 vols., London, 1909–14). For an up-to-date and thorough study of the late empire, the student can now consult A. H. M. Jones, *The Later Roman Empire, 248–602 A.D.* (3 vols., Oxford, 1964). *The Decline of the Ancient World* (London, 1966) is a shortened and simplified version of this work. Another work of fundamental importance is Fergus Millar's *The Roman Empire and Its Neighbors* (London, 1967). There are several good one-volume studies of Roman history: A. E. R. Boak and W. G. Sinnigen, *History of Rome to 565 A.D.* (5th ed., New York, 1965); M. Cary and H. H. Scullard, *A History of Rome* (3rd ed., New York, 1976); and F. M. Heichelheim and C. A. Yeo, *A History of the Roman People* (Englewood Cliffs, New Jersey, 1962). For the early imperial period, a detailed narrative account is provided by J. B. Bury's *A History of the Roman Empire from Its Foundation to the Death of Marcus Aurelius (27 B.C.–180 A.D.)*, (London, 1900). A brief but excellent account of the first three centuries of the empire is to be found in M. P. Charlesworth's *The Roman Empire* (London, 1951). The fourth century is usually treated in connection with the problem of transition to the Middle Ages, but there are several special studies of it. Piganiol's *L'Empire Chrétien* (Paris, 1947) gives a detailed and thorough account. Another useful one-volume treatment of the late empire is H. M. D. Parker's *A History of the Roman World from A.D. 138 to 337*, rev. by B. H. Warmington (London, 1969).

Our understanding of Roman social history has come a long way since the pioneering work of Samuel Dill, *Roman Society in the Last Century of the Western Empire* (2nd ed., London, 1899). Some of the most interesting work is that of Ramsay MacMullen in a series of monographs: *Soldier and Civilian in the Later Roman Empire* (Cambridge, Mass., 1967); *Enemies of the Roman Order* (Cambridge, Mass., 1966); *Roman Social Relations, 50 B.C. to A.D. 284* (New Haven, 1974); *Roman Governments' Response to Crisis, A.D. 285–337* (New Haven, 1976). For an understanding of intellectual life in the empire, T. R. Glover's *Life and Literature in the Fourth Century* (Cambridge, 1901) and C. G. Starr's *Civilization and the Caesars: The Intellectual Revolution in the Roman Empire* (Ithaca, 1954) are useful. Sir Ronald Syme's *Ammianus and the Historia Augusta* (Oxford, 1968), Alan Cameron's

Claudian (Oxford, 1970), and Jay Bregman's *Synesius of Cyrene, Philosopher Bishop* (Berkeley, 1982) are more recent studies of important figures in the intellectual life of the late empire.

The problem of transition from the ancient to the medieval world has received much attention. The first two volumes of the *Cambridge Medieval History* (2nd ed., Cambridge, 1936) contain detailed studies by specialists. A good narrative is provided by J. B. Bury, *History of the Later Roman Empire, 395–565* (2 vols., London, 1923). The idea that there was any "decline" or "fall" or "ruin" was challenged by Ferdinand Lot, *The End of the Ancient World and the Beginning of the Middle Ages* (New York, 1931). Alfons Dopsch, in *The Economic and Social Foundations of European Civilization* (New York, 1937), argued on behalf of unbroken cultural and economic continuity from the later Roman Empire into the Carolingian period. The thesis of Henri Pirenne's *Mohammed and Charlemagne* (London, 1939) is that such continuity was present until the Islamic conquest of the Mediterranean. Other helpful studies include R. F. Arragon's *The Transition from the Ancient to the Medieval World* (New York, 1936); H. St.-L. B. Moss, *The Birth of the Middle Ages, 395–814* (2nd ed., London, 1947); and Solomon Katz, *The Decline of Rome and the Rise of Medieval Europe* (Ithaca, 1955). Valuable contributions to the discussion have been made more recently by a collection of essays edited by Lynn White, *The Transformations of the Roman World: Gibbon's Problem after Two Centuries* (Berkeley and Los Angeles, 1966) and by Peter Brown's *The World of Late Antiquity,* A.D. *150–750* (London, 1971), an excerpt from which is included in this volume.

The literature of the various interpretations of Rome's fall is enormous. A. Demandt's *Der Fall Roms. Die Auflösung des römischen Reiches im Urteil der Nachwelt* (Munich, 1984) devotes a thick volume to a survey of all the theories published up to our time. The following represents only a sampling. Some are basically political: K. J. Beloch's, "Der Verfall der antiken Kultur," *Historische Zeitschrift* 84 (1900), argues that by absorbing the Greek city-states, the Roman Empire stifled the creative forces of antiquity. E. Kornemann's "Das Problem des Untergangs der antiken Walt," *Vergangenheit und Gegenwart* 12 (1922): 193–202 and 241–54, blames Rome's fall on the reduction of the military force by Augustus. G. Ferrero, in his *La Ruine de la civilisation antique* (Paris, 1921), believes that by returning to the hereditary principle and appointing his son Commodus to the throne,

Marcus Aurelius undermined the authority of the senate and the basis of the Roman state. W. E. Heitland's thesis, set forth in *The Roman Fate* (Cambridge, 1922) is also political in its emphasis. He elaborated it in two subsequent pamphlets, *Iterum, or a Further Discussion of the Roman Fate* (Cambridge, 1925) and *Last Words on the Roman Municipalities* (Cambridge, 1928).

To the category of economic and social explanation belong the selections from Rostovtzeff, Walbank, and Baynes. At the center of many of such explanations is the failure of antiquity to develop modern forms of industry and economic organization. An explanation for this failure is offered by K. Bucher, *Die Entstehung der Volkwirtschaft* (16th ed., Tubingen, 1922); G. Salvioli, *Il capitalismo antico* (Bari, 1929); and M. Weber, "Wirtschaft und Gesellschaft," *Grundriss der Soziolokonomik* (1921): 221 ff. They contend that ancient industry could not develop because the ancient world never emerged from the stage of house-economy to the heights of city-economy and state-economy. Their position is challenged by Rostovtzeff in his article, "The Decay of the Ancient World and Its Economic Explanation," *Economic History Review* 2 (1939): 197 ff. In the same category would fall the theory of V. G. Simkhovitch, "Rome's Fall Reconsidered," *Political Science Quarterly* 31 (1916): 201–43, presenting the argument in favor of exhaustion of the soil as a factor, and that of Ellsworth Huntington, "Climatic Change and Agricultural Exhaustion as Elements in the Fall of Rome," *Quarterly Journal of Economics* 31 (February 1917): 173 ff. The economic experiences of the twentieth century have given rise to some other economic suggestions for Rome's fall, such as L. C. West's in "The Economic Collapse of the Roman Empire," *Classical Journal* 26 (1931): 96 ff., and W. D. Gray, "The Roman Depression and Our Own," *Classical Journal* 29 (1934): 243 ff.

Various interpretations of a biological nature have also been put forth. Tenney Frank's essay "Race Mixture in the Roman Empire," *American Historical Review* 21 (July 1916): 689–708, argued that the decline of Rome resulted from "the fact that the people who built Rome had given way to a different race." The factual basis of his theory, the distribution of foreign names on Roman gravestones, has been challenged by M. L. Gordon, "The Nationality of Slaves under the Early Roman Empire," *Journal of Roman Studies* 14 (1924): 93–111. Another version of the biological explanation is that of O. Seeck, *Geschichte des Untergangs der antiken Welt* (Berlin 1901), who sees as the cause of Rome's collapse the "extermination of the best" among its citizens by foreign and civil wars. Some, like Oswald Spengler, *The Decline of the West* (2 vols., London, 1926–1928), believe that all societies are overtaken by natural decay.

The theory that Christianity was to blame was held by many pagans who survived Alaric's sack of Rome in 410 and brought forth apologetic responses by the Christians, among them Saint Augustine. Gibbon hinted broadly at such an explanation in several passages. The idea has not won wide support, yet it keeps recurring in one form or another. An attempt to revitalize it with an injection of Marxism was made by G. Sorel, *La Ruine du monde antique* (Paris, 1925). As Rostovtzeff said, "This book is without value for the historian." Still, so sober and excellent a historian as Michael Grant, in an excerpt included in this volume and elsewhere in his *The Fall of the Roman Empire: A Reappraisal* (London, 1976), argues that Christianity played an important, but not unique, role in undermining the defense of Roman culture. The study of the place of Christianity in the Roman world, therefore, remains important. Valuable contributions to this field include M. L. W. Laistner, *Christianity and Pagan Culture in the Later Roman Empire* (Ithaca, 1951); E. A. Goodenough, *The Church in the Roman Empire* (New York, 1931); A. Momigliano, ed., *The Conflict between Paganism and Christianity* (Oxford, 1963); and E. R. Dodds, *Pagan and Christian in an Age of Anxiety* (Cambridge, 1965). Peter Brown's *Augustine of Hippo* is a particularly valuable study of a key figure. Ramsay MacMullen has also studied the place of religion in the empire in two volumes, *Paganism in the Roman Empire* (New Haven, 1981) and *Christianizing the Roman Empire* (New Haven, 1984). More recently he examined the role played by venality in *Corruption and the Decline of Rome* (New Haven, 1988).

The recent revival of military history has produced studies like those by Luttwak and Ferrill included in this volume.

Arnold Toynbee treats Rome's decline in the fourth volume of his *A Study of History* (Oxford, 1936), where he deals with the problem of decline in general. A more recent book by R. M. Haywood, *The Myth of Rome's Fall* (New York, 1958), returns to something like Bury's view. To the questions Can we learn something of the future by our study of the Roman Empire? and Will that study not yield some great secret of civilization?, Haywood answers No, we may expect the answers only to "innumerable minor ones." However that may be, it is nonetheless necessary to continue asking the major ones.